word west revue

isbn: 979-8-9893940-4-3

published by word west

first us edition 2023

printed in the usa

wordwest.co

cover & interior design: word west

cover image: charles o'rear

type: migra (pangram pangram)

vol. 1

word west revue

<table>
<tr><td>

Editors

David Byron Queen
Colin Winnette
Lauren Lavín
Gwen Nicholson
Dani Putney
Hattie Hayes
Sawyer Elms
Karthik Sethuraman
Robin Bissett
Matt Mitchell
Kylie Westerlind
Mackenzie Moore
M. Price
Yunya Yang
Franco Romero

</td><td>

Readers

Claire Audrey Aguayo
Sarah Marie Lowe
Lanie Nowak
Taylor Cuccia
Charles G. Thompson
Debbie Williams
Harrison Cook

</td></tr>
</table>

Special Thanks To:
Alex Higley, Jake Longstreth, Pangram Pangram

Nocturne

Kate Finegan

valley

I dreamed I had swallowed a tooth and woke up with a sore throat, as if the bone-sharp incisor had fought its way down my esophagus. My partner was still asleep, sweating as he did all night every night, and as I lay there with his dampness in the canvas tent-cabin where we lived together, technically roommates, fellow rangers, I ran my index finger over all my teeth and felt no gaps. Wind shook the canvas walls like sheets on a line, and I fell in and out of sleep, dreaming I was in a small boat on choppy seas, and every whitecap was a molar, and when the wave crashed, the tooth melted to water. When he woke up, I told him what I'd dreamed, and he said, "Babe, I'm not even through my first cup" and the instant coffee smelled of earth, and I had the strongest urge to strip naked, go outside, and spin and spin and spin and spin inside the circle of these rippling canvas-sided cabins, all filled with park employees, to see if somehow my feet could bore themselves down into the morning moistness, the loamy soil, and then my ankles, calves, and thighs, and everything. I didn't mention this to him.

My sister, through a bad connection, said dreaming of swallowing a tooth meant maybe I was pregnant, so I drove out of the park and wandered all around the nearest dollar store, up one aisle, down the other, until I realized the tests were by the register, as if someone would see them and think *I guess I am feeling a little bloated, and I guess I am a little late* and count back twenty-eight and balance the impulse-buy in their full hands, atop the paper towels, Campbell's soup, and six-pack. The girl at the register, no older than eighteen, smiled much too long at me after ringing the purchase through. "Good luck," she said. All I did was grunt.

"It's negative," I told my partner over scrambled eggs I'd burned in the shared kitchen of our canvas tent-cabin compound, and he said, "Huh?" and I said, "Nothing, never mind," and pulled out my papers on New Zealand Mud Snails for a talk I was developing, a cautionary talk on how to stem the spread of these invasives.

A little girl asked if a snail could change its shell. I told her the shell grows along with its soft body.

She asked if a snail is born inside its shell. I told her yes, it is. Her brother asked if a snail has teeth. I told him snails have rows and rows of teeth, and when a row wears down, a new one grows to fill its place. The girl asked if a snail can mend its shell, because her brother liked to crush them. I said yes, because it's true they can mend small holes, but a crushed shell, all that broken calcium, means death. I couldn't tell her that.

My partner became my ex, but not before he forced himself on me. The park superintendent was a man who'd been transferred from another park for groping women on their interviews, so I didn't even try to get my not-yet-ex moved, not after we'd begged and pleaded for this canvas shack together. That's why I was the one to move, when another so-called cabin had an open space. I took all my stuff over while he led a guided hike. My new roommate warned me her hamster would run laps on its wheel all night, and I would come to learn she wasn't lying. Afterwards, I saw my ex in the dining hall. He swiped his card and sat down where we always sat. I swiped my card and left with gummy pasta that made me feel my mouth was mush.

My sister nearly missed her connection due to a coyote on the runway but deplaned resplendent, with an issue of *Cosmopolitan* and a bottle of duty-free tequila. "Happy housewarming!" she said, and I laughed because it was just the next cabin over, and my ex and I still shared a bathhouse. But my roommate left the valley for a wedding, so my sister had a bed to sleep in as she helped me to survive the break-up. We didn't speak of trauma, of what he had tried to do to me. We annotated the shitty magazine, all its shitty sex tricks, like we'd done when we were kids, when I was much too young to be cackling at the concept of surprise prostate stimulation. I told her New Zealand Mud Snails reproduce asexually, so all it takes is one, and she said, "New Zealand what?" We got tequila-drunk. She held my hair as I puked, held me close as the hamster wheel whirred and rattled, and in the morning, my teeth looked yellow in the bathhouse mirror. My sister stepped out of the shower in her towel and caught me grimacing at my reflection. "Huh?" she said. "I dreamed my teeth were rotten." I brushed so hard my gums bled then gave a talk on life that scurries through the park at night.

transience

Since then, so many parks, so many lakes and rivers, mountains and canyons, because the truth is I never could relax again, not in the valley, not in that tent of rippling canvas, in that ring of tents that glowed white like luminescent teeth, where I dreamed my incisor crumbled and a soft snail body oozed to fill the cracks. I was adrift in a world of seasonal work, moving place to place, into tiny cabins and shared dorm rooms, old run-down farmhouses with bedroom doors with broken locks. Every national park was America's best idea, so wasn't it all worth it, even if wasps nested in my closet, even if the shower only ran ice-cold, even if one roommate, a veteran of Operation Enduring Freedom, sleep-walked, reliving flashbacks, and once came into my room at night and woke me from a dream of dentures by lying down beside me and sweating in his night terrors, and wouldn't *you* have let him sleep, knowing what *you* knew about the trauma he had gone through, and wouldn't *you* have given him the benefit of the doubt, the space to heal, until he pinned your arms down in the morning and laughed when you finally, finally freed yourself from his vise grip? That night, you'd dream of scorpions. You'd dream you laughed as you pushed him off of you, like it was all a joke, and a scorpion dangled from the tip of your tongue, which was pierced through by its pincer. At least, that's what *I* dreamed after it happened, and when I woke up, I had an email—I was being transferred to the desert.

desert

I dreamed I ground my teeth to powder. Each morning, I'd bite down on scrambled egg or muffin, soft, and swear I was eating my own sand. The dentist said *that's not a dream* and prescribed a night guard. I dreamed of blueprints, that contractors erected scaffolding behind my lips then toy soldiers with power tools and paintbrushes instead of guns were raised by pulley to my teeth, which needed fixing, and then the dream went dark, and all that lived within my cabin in a valley named for death was buzz of drill and pound of hammer, shellac-swish to bind my teeth in place.

The desert came alive at night, and so did we. We'd gather outside the cabins to drink heady homebrew from a man with a Civil War mustache; we'd dance with an audience of glowing eyes, unblinking from the darkness, as creatures came to bid us well, and my bed was rarely empty, and as I slept beside the man I'd marry, I could feel the tug as an owl-dentist with its owl-eyes magnified still further yanked my teeth out one-by-one with talons. We flew my sister to Las Vegas as our witness, lost so much money at the slots, and married in a chapel favored by B-list celebrities. It was beautiful, and after, we watched stars fall all around us from the casino's rooftop pool until we stumbled back to bed. When I dreamed that I was giving a talk on how animals find water in the desert and kept pausing to spit teeth one-by-one into my palms until both hands filled up, and the campfire-circle children took them and roasted them on sticks so they puffed up, I rolled over to hold my new husband, and when that didn't soothe me into sleep, I knocked on my sister's door, and climbed into bed beside her, and she held me like we were kids, and I outslept my hangover and woke to old music on the radio, the sort we'd listen to with a cassette tape in, waiting for our favorite song to play so we could hit record and save that song forever.

When I turned out to be truly pregnant, my dreams did not portend it. Instead, I had a string of dreamless nights that turned into bloodless days, and when I bought the pregnancy test, my husband was there beside me, and he held it in his hand as the two lines appeared. I sent my sister all the metaphors—*the fetus is now the size of a fig*—and she would text back, *weird.* I sent them as a joke, but I did feel perhaps there was some unruly life inside me, something beyond the growth of cells that would one day live and walk and breathe outside my body. I dreamed my mouth swelled with the progression of the fruits, until I couldn't speak, until I could scarcely swallow, and I woke to sharp-then-throbbing pain, a strobe light of it, and my husband drove the many miles to the nearest hospital, dodging coyotes and jackrabbits on the ribbon of road that ran through their nighttime thoroughfares, and the doctors said I didn't have a fever, said I didn't seem to be in any danger.

But the pain persisted, and I dreamed I tried to bite into the fruits my child was becoming and couldn't and couldn't and couldn't because my teeth would wobble in my gums, until I twisted out the two teeth front-and-center and whistled when I talked. I told my sister, and she called the doctor for me, and the doctor said she couldn't talk to her to protect my privacy, but she said I should come in for an ultrasound, so I did, and the doctor didn't want to show me pictures, just the text of the report, but eventually I got them—images of a tooth inside my left ovary, seemingly tethered to my little fruit by the fallopian tube. I dreamed my child reached out little arms and wound up the fallopian tube like an extension cord or leash or lasso and held the tooth to its chest. Then I dreamed the child swallowed it, swallowed this wayward tooth.

My sister talked to her own doctor, who said this sort of thing is not uncommon. Sometimes it's teeth, sometimes it's hair, sometimes it's even bones and skin. I couldn't get the dermoid cyst removed, not with the life ripening inside of me. An extraction would be too dangerous, so it grew alongside my child. I could have given a program on it—how this tooth sprang from the same cells as the egg that would grow into a human. Likely, it arose from the cells that were left over from the development of that very ovum. Under the right conditions, this tooth could have been another life. So much comes down to right conditions, to right environment. I had to sit down, out-of-breath, so often. I sweated through my wool-and-polyester uniform. The light glinting off the sand could blind me with a headache. I vomited from pain then smiled my way through a talk on desert pupfish, resilient creatures the size of a baby's pinkie-finger, which survived the massive shrinking and salinization of their ancient lake to survive the hot-water springs and desert streams that eons of change have left them with; cut off from others of their species, they've formed distinct and dazzling sub-species. Even when I went on leave, when the dermoid cyst made even these campground talks too painful, I kept reading about the strange life of this isolated place. My husband held me close through all of it, microwaved packets of plain rice when that was all I could keep down. When I read that the Badwater snail is the size of a grain of rice, I dreamed rice crunched like snail shells when I ate it, and the snails stitched their shells back together and came to life inside my womb. My husband squeezed lemons into water, did all he could to tame the nausea.

I called my sister every day. She told me it would be okay. She told me the child wouldn't come out cradling this invasive tooth. She told me the tooth wouldn't grow into my child's chest, wouldn't lodge into my child's head, wouldn't cut me on its way out.

My husband gave a program on the food chain of the desert. He ordered owl pellets online, had them shipped to the park office. I think they came from Illinois, a sham. But the children loved it. And when I was nearly due and couldn't bear to be alone for all my fear about delivery, fear of water breaking and the baby flooding out, all covered in teeth, I went with him, unpaid, to help. I showed the children how to slice open the oblong mass of refuse, to extract what the owl spit up from its living, wriggling meal—the bones, the keratin of claws, the hair. I opened up my pellet, and there it was—a tooth, so perfect and so smooth. I held onto that tooth, thought to string it on a necklace chain, but after a night of dreams in which the wayward tooth inside me gnawed its way out through my navel, I placed it on the steps outside our cabin and, with the heel of my park boots, I crushed it. I don't know if I dreamt it, but I think I felt the baby kick when that sharp tooth turned to powder.

Never Looked Better

Lindsay Hunter

She's looking in the mirror. On your good days, you imagine she sees bags under her eyes, puffy cheeks from those pills you've read about, and those pink drinks you can't afford, teeth too white and square, wad of gum perpetually wadded, smudged eye makeup, ratty margarine-colored extensions. You pretend she hates herself as much as you hate yourself. As much as you hate her. So rich, so lucky! This morning you discovered your dog had peed inside your shoe, the left one of the pair you bought at Payless because you squinted and convinced yourself they looked nice, though at home they were dull, not shiny, the toes rounded, making you think of the way you used to round your shoulders and retreat at recess, parties, work. Used to. Britney has dogs, and her frayed hems and knotted underhairs make you think surely that's happened to her, surely one of her platform slides smells like animal, but she snaps her manicured fingers and someone with rounded shoulders comes and cleans it for her. Buys her new shoes. Buys her a new house, a new dog. You had to soak your shoe in hot water and dish soap, the cheap kind, thin, no bubbles, because the good dish soap was out of your budget that week. You can't afford new shoes. You can't even afford new shoe. You slopped through a shift at Red Lobster two towns over in that shoe, and it was far from the worst part of your day. The drive with the tank past empty. The dead lobster belly up in the aquarium right by the door. The fogged water that clung to your arm as you lifted it out. That stupid shoe was third, fourth.

Britney's on all the magazine covers. Everywhere you go, she sees you. She sees all of you. Britney's In Love! those covers bleat. You wonder if you've ever truly been in love. You think of the boy that put one finger under your chin and the other wiggling in between the buttons of your shirt. You got a fat little tummy, he said. Britney wonders the same exact thing. You're in love with her, or the closest thing to it. You, all of you, the way you obsess over her. Her nude body, flashing stars off her hips. No, just a flesh-colored body suit and rhinestones. Still, you imagine. A man asks her on live television about her breasts. My breasts, she repeats, the way teenagers do when you ask them something dumbfounding. My grades? My friends? My job? My breasts. Britney laughs; it's funny! Right? She looks offscreen, maybe hoping to see defiance, rage, in her assistant Felicia's eyes. Instead she sees the same dumb giggle. Haw haw. She went back that night and stabbed that man in his ear with his own monogrammed letter opener, collected the blood and brain matter in her Versace Medusa. If you stay past the encore, you can watch the lights go out one by one. Then you're in total blackness. She stayed until he knew what she meant. Here you go, Fe, she said, handing over the bag the next morning. You work so hard.

Now she's on a private jet and where are you? In your shitty hatchback on your way back to Red Lobster. You hate the dayshift, you hate your stacked block apartment on Chipeta and that you will return to it. Britney smells like an old bra and you smell like you walked through the breezeway of a Bath & Body Works a hundred times. Four hundred times. Clouds like a massive fluffy carpet rolled out for her. You hear the engine of a passing plane above and you see yourself in your rearview mirror and you look like someone is pressing you down, pushing you into the ground. Buried.

There are stories you've heard and you don't know if they're true but they're fun to consider. Britney is high all the time, those lavender pills that cost a year's paycheck for you; Britney has sex with whomever; Britney died and was replaced by a lookalike with brain damage. Britney put a hit out on her father. Britney cries every night because she misses home, misses her family. You cried the other night because you couldn't afford to eat; you'd have to wait until the dinner shift and hope your manager Terry takes pity on you, doesn't punch in your order but just hands over the plate and waves you away. You don't have enough even with your employee discount. Has Britney ever felt that?

You don't know this for sure, but some part of you knows: Britney killed a photographer that wouldn't stop following her. Lured him by letting him follow her, whipping around the curves in the Canyon, driving wildly, driving herself, she used to know someone who lived up there, that home that looks so cozy and clean all lit up at night, but he hurt her bad and thinking of it makes her sick to her stomach in the car. Her driver wanted to drive her, she is repeating this sentence over and over because it's fun, it's sort of musical; she is a musician. Her driver wanted to drive her, repeat. Her foot has pushed the gas pedal to the floor. If she dies at least her story will finally have an end. Instead she's driving right up to the edge of a cliff, the paparazzo on her tail, accelerating into the promise of a photo, the photo, and at the last second Britney turns and he doesn't. He sails right off the edge. Beautiful, really. She thinks she can hear his car burst into flames, but there is always roaring in her ears. Applause, feedback, terror. It's all the same to her, now. The man had a fiancée and a tiny daughter who just had her ears pierced. Britney feels nothing.

You don't even like that song, the one that came out about her. Melodramatic and tedious. You wonder how she feels about it. You imagine she is steel inside when it comes to him, her first. You don't know that he is a bore, that he wanted constant reassurance from her, that he made her hold his penis like a mother holding her nervous child's hand.

You have only ever been cheated on. You've never been the cheater. You hate these other women, these whores. They are better than you, aren't they? They are. They are all Britneys and you, you don't even have a name. Britney's name is like two neat stabs, choreographed and rehearsed and on their marks. Swishing sharply away before the blood even runs. One boy you loved, though. You aren't aware of what Britney knows, that love is a game of pretend and inevitably it gets tiring for one of the players. He just stopped talking to you, like you were something he imagined and he'd pivoted to a different creation. You were supposed to evaporate, to cease, but you couldn't and you can't. Hard as you try, because you're a dumb bitch and you're not even cool enough to say that part out loud.

Britney is a human being and she makes mistakes. Britney just wants to fall in love, fall right through the floor and keep on falling, past where those long camera lenses can find her. If she can just smear an eraser over herself. She knows she can't become anyone else but she can ruin what is there. It is no longer possible to keep all of herself together. Every day she watches another little bit departiculate or unarticulate or whatever word Oprah would use is, watches it flutter off like the butterfly on her back and that is smeared too. At clubs people hear her yelling FUCK IT and WOOOO and YEAH but they don't hear the rage, a tone which hovers above human hearing. She lets the cameras take her picture, take and take and take and take. She shows them her face, her creation, how it no longer does what it's told. Her eyes change; now they stare into flashes without blinking, those great black pools that reflect back what they see, which is you, staring, grimacing, searching, laughing that mean laugh. You like what you see because you hate what you see. It's you. Britney is you.

Next she kills a bartender she fucked. He fell down her spiral staircase. He fell, she says, in her baby voice. I see, says the cop, but he is wondering about her breasts. It wasn't his fault, she thinks, but she can't remember the reason. She kills her cook, just pushes his face right down into the vat of oil he's boiling for her favorite fried chicken. He lets her, it's heartbreaking how little he fights. He's erect as he dies. She kills Leeza Gibbons, strangling her in the shadows of a red carpet, who is replaced by a lookalike, brain damage, before the first award is given out. Britney has people. Her people have people.

Then: where did he come from? He's rangy and he has dimples and he smiles at her the way everyone smiled at each other in church when she was a girl. Anonymous and polite. It reminds her of something she'd long forgotten. She never figured out what that was. Girl, her assistant says, halfheartedly, already on the walkie about troubleshooting this one. They drink and they fuck and he knows about drugs, she lets him think he knows more than she does. This one, she kisses. She didn't know kissing could be a search, find me, find me. He tries harder than anyone before. Or maybe not, maybe he was just as blank as a kite and she flew him and she was also the wind and it felt the way she wanted it to feel. It is hard to know if she is the world or if the world is a projector on a big blank wall. She has his babies, it is so fun to have his babies inside her. She doesn't kill for nine months and that lasts through the next pregnancy. She has them so close together. A blessing, everyone tells her. A blessing, a blessing, she's nodding and nodding and the tears coat her face. Aw, they say, aw.

You have kids, too. The cook at work is nice, and he stays until morning, and so what if he can't have a driver's license. We all have issues, don't we? Before you even figure out if you wanted the first baby another comes along. They feel like invasions, like someone hooked up a hose to your chest and turned on the vacuum. You check your bank account, you check again. They'll eat but you won't and it's fine, it'll be fine. The cook moved three states away, because there's work there, something with construction. He doesn't own boots or a hammer, it's his brother's company or a friend of his brother's company. Who knows? Not him. A woman downstairs watches the boys when you're at work, and you're always at work, and when you pick them up the woman is enraged and the boys are so sleepy, so sweet and warm and sleepy. Does Britney walk around feeling like this? This blanket of fear that something will happen, that something always happens, that the illusion of any order in the universe is just a card trick. Ask for help, the articles say before your laptop dies. So simple! I am asking for help, you think. You haven't showered in weeks. You cling to them, your babies, because making sure they know they're loved, even if it's a desperate, brackish, terrified love, is a mother's only allowable violence. The TV is too loud and that's something you can fix but you've forgotten how.

The nannies smile at Britney's children in a way that makes her desperate, too. Is she jealous of her boys? I'm their mother, she reminds them. I'm their mother, she hisses at her assistant, her own mother, an interviewer from a third-rate magazine who buzzes at her gate. Yes you are, darlin, says her assistant, but she's hidden her mouth behind her hand. Where's Daddy? someone is asking. Where's Daddy? Britney repeats. One of the nannies smiles at her and Britney smiles back even as she hits the woman, hits her again, can't stop hitting her, the baby thinks it's funny and she keeps going. Babe, her assistant says, babe come on now. That felt good, Britney says, out of breath, like the old days when she'd hop off the stage into the cool darkness and it'd finally be over, until the next one. She dials his number and he picks up and he says he was at the store, that she sent him for juice and brownie bites, but wasn't that days ago? She tries to say something to her assistant. Tries to prep her by saying, I am about to say something. What day is it? is what she says, but her assistant is already turning, already laughing. It feels better when she is on the floor with the children, when she is really in it, when she is playing blocks or reading books about a grumpy fish but she looks up and only three minutes have passed. WHAT WILL YOU DO WITH YOUR LIFE? she remembers her pastor booming at them when she was a child. What will you do with the life God has given you? It used to make her feel an urgency but now she knows the answer doesn't matter. God? she thinks. God? She lets an interviewer touch her, smothers him with her thighs. Begs her assistant to keep him, put him in the case with the gleaming awards, but it's another no. God never answers. She's never looked better, they all say after her appearance on a late show. She's back, they crow. But I was never even here, she thinks. All liars.

You've figured something out. One day you look at your oldest boy's shoulders, so tiny, his perfect posture, the delicate lines of his neck, and you want someone to come and do something, protect him, take him somewhere safe. And you hear a voice and maybe it's Britney's and it's saying, That's you. That's your job. And from that day forward it is your job. You surrender. You go on food stamps and you take one less shift and you water down the milk, let yourself eat half a sandwich a day, because it's what you can do. Let's go to the library, you say. Let's go to the park. You hand them strawberries, frozen because they're cheaper. You become that thing everyone warns against, that pitied and embarrassing thing. You become a mother, and the secret is that you've never felt more powerful in your life. They grow and grow and they're polite and curious and impossibly sweet and when they talk back or say No! you are sure you're doing something right, because you're not a weed choking the life out of them, you're the sun and water and air and they flourish. Your pockets are filled with wrappers and pebbles and snotty tissue. You feel a sort of communion with the natural order of things, but every once in a while, you strut. You start to think maybe this is better than everything she has, everything you thought you wanted. Smoothing your kid's cowlick, offering a Band-Aid, there you are, forgetting to covet her.

You see pictures of Britney. She almost drops her baby. She's crying in a restaurant, seated right by the window, clutching her child. Someone help her, you think. Then you remember she's rich enough to have all the help she could stand and your boy wants a string cheese and you forget all about it. You smell like seafood blend out of a plastic bag but you don't smell anything.

Britney's head hurts. It always hurts so fucking bad. The doctor gives her pills the size of gumballs but still it throbs. She can't hear what anyone is saying. Roaring. Her teeth push against each other, the only way to distract from the pain. Sweetie, it's these nasty extensions, someone says one night. He's got his fingers in them, examining. Honey, this is a crime, he says. He's shouting and she can't hear him but she figured out how to read lips long ago. Come to the salon, he says. But she doesn't know which one. She finds one and it's closed but an ugly woman lets her in. It smells like the hairspray of her childhood and the walls seem to hold the roar of hair dryers in a yellowy hush and the woman says No, I won't do that, so Britney does it herself. It's nice to remember she can do some things by herself. See, Britney says to the woman, who isn't ugly, just plain, and Britney almost cries she is so happy to see a face that hasn't been surgically adjusted, See, she says and hurries out the door and leaves the woman to wonder what exactly it is Britney Spears smells like, is it body odor or takeout or some new expensive perfume she doesn't understand, and years later she will realize what it was, it was decay. Britney takes a taxi home. The driver clucks and says it's a shame, what she's done to herself. Says it like he owns a part of her and maybe he does. She pushes the pen she stole from the salon into the driver's neck and leaves the door open as she walks away. Where are her boys? She has to find out. Her head doesn't hurt anymore, does it?

The whole world is saying they're concerned but they're saying it behind their hands. She's fine because she has the money to be just fine. At one point everyone has felt envious of her and for that she's paying an appropriate price. The Leeza Gibbons clone wonders if it has something to do with postpartum depression and the man next to her clamps his hand over her mouth. How dare you, he grits, motherhood is a gift. Then it's too late, they all talk about how she needs help. Britney Needs Help, sources cry out. Not sexy, not pretty, like she doesn't care if we want to fuck her or not. Kill her, they start to think. She should die.

If she survives, she'll show up wearing next to nothing again, just the way you like her. You'll all pause and stare at her abdomen, at her thighs, at the return of those extensions. Sometimes she'll make a triumphant return. The next one will be a disaster. The one after that will be nostalgic, filled with grace. But it all depends on you. It all depends on what you're willing to allow. You're aging, so why does she have to?

You scroll and zoom. If you're feeling even that day, you'll comfort yourself. She must have gotten help, you'll think. I'm glad she got help.

How to Swallow a Canyon

Katie Manning

after Frank X. Walker

Write down that word your mom said when you were 12:
_________ *are the most disgusting.*

Look up the etymology of *disgust*—
try to *reverse* your *taste*.

Light your Grand Canyon candle souvenir.

Watch the flame make the flute player dance beside
a rainbow
in silence.

Hold your mother's word over the fire—
but don't ignite it.

You still can't bring yourself to answer.

Secret Name

Justin Taylor

They stop trying after the second time. Ten weeks was hard enough, but eighteen—and they'd already told Tess' parents and Bern's mom. It's too much. After just long enough that it doesn't seem causal, though it is absolutely causal, they adopt a three-legged cat named Samson, a five-year-old orange short-hair with white front paws.

It's the left hind leg that's missing. The people at the adoption place don't know what happened, only that the small clean scar is indicative of surgery rather than trauma, which in turn suggests some illness or injury in his past. This is enough to make Bern nervous ("Will we really want to go through all that again?" he asks, not specifying what "all that" is, not even conscious that he's said "again") but Tess has the cat in her arms and a certain look in her eye. "Little mittens, like the nursery rhyme," she says.

Bern defers.

Samson is still skittish, but settling, it seems, into the new digs. It's been nine days now, or ten, Bern doesn't remember, which itself is a good thing, right? To no longer be counting by the day. It is Friday afternoon and Tess is packing an overnight bag. She is a yoga instructor with a three-year A.A. chip and a burgeoning Instagram presence. Her first photo of Samson curled up on their couch garnered nearly a thousand hearts. This weekend she is leading a retreat out on the Oregon coast. Breath work and stretches. Sunrise swims and vegetarian lunch on the big back deck of the hotel. Extra-long savasana (corpse pose) to end the evening sessions. Many if not most of her clients will enjoy a glass of white wine while they take in the sunset on the cooling sand. She will not begrudge them this. She will practice mindfulness, which, among other things, will mean not picturing the tsunami that will appear eighteen minutes after the century-overdue earthquake described in that article that everyone was talking about last summer. People she'd gone to high school with and hadn't spoken to since were posting it and tagging her, asking if she was okay, as though the disaster had already happened, as though it were happening now.

But if it were to happen, it is true that the coast would be the worst place for a person to be. A veritable death sentence: the tsunami zone. Forget all that. Tess will ward off apocalypse with simple thoughts articulated slowly, steady as yogic breathing: *The sunset is pretty on the water,* she'll think. *It is nice that it is cooler here than back in Portland.* The theme she has chosen for the weekend is "Rootedness to the earth." She's complained to Bern that some of her Insta-fans have found this confusing. Why not "flow" for water, they ask, or "change" for shifting sand? She has had to remind them that sand and water too are parts of the earth.

She should have been on the road twenty minutes ago, she's telling him now. She shouldn't be the last one to arrive at her own retreat.

Bern and the cat are both in the home office. Bern's working and Samson is curled up next to his laptop, having claimed the computer's soft-sided case for a daybed. She kisses them each in turn—the cat on its head, Bern on his mouth—and admonishes them to stay cool, keep each other company, and have fun on their "boys' weekend."

"Ten-four," Bern says, turning back to his computer, the afterimage of her kiss still tingling on his stubbly lip. "Lock the door behind me," she calls from the living room.

The whole Northwest is having a heat wave. It was ninety-seven degrees when they got up this morning, hit a hundred at noon and still climbing. Numbers all but unheard of for this region, at least until these last few years. Bern and Tess have talked about what it means if this is the new normal. Would you even want to bring a child into a world like that?

Bern has all the shades down and the A/C blasting. When he next gets up he'll make a pit-stop in the kitchen to double-check that Samson's water dish is full.

Bern had wanted to change the cat's name, indeed was going to make it a condition of his yielding on the question of adopting *this* cat rather than some other, healthier animal; and Tess had been about to give him the go-ahead (he's sure of this) but then the lady at the shelter butted in to tell them how much better it would be for Samson's "adjustment" if he had "continuity." And that, naturally, was all Tess needed to hear. Well, Bern thinks, it does seem to have paid off insofar as Samson *has* adjusted. He slept at Bern's feet last night, which fact Tess noted over breakfast. So effusively and at such length that Bern realized she was jealous.

Bern works in tech. He works from home and has a hard time explaining his job to people, but when pressed, which he rarely is, he will say that though he is not a programmer he speaks the language of programmers, serving as a sort of ambassador between their world of arcane jargon and higher math to that of the suits, the men—and they are all men—who think in broad, glittering concepts and want their products to work as if by magic, to be received as miracle, which Bern believes is precisely what most people believe that most technology is. He even allows himself to believe this, albeit in a limited, provisional way. The washing machine orders its own soap refill; his wristwatch knows his blood pressure and his name.

He's finished with work for today, thankfully. Next item on the agenda is to receive the guy from the HVAC company, who is coming to give an estimate on replacing the house's duct work, which is down in the crawlspace and all rusted out. They've been meaning to deal with this for two years now; it was on the inspection report when they bought the place, and has only gotten worse, but it was one of those things that always somehow got bumped down the to-do list (it's not like you can *see* ductwork) until the confluent arrival of the heat wave and the cat.

Bern is thinking he might start calling the cat Samus, after the protagonist of the *Metroid* video game franchise, which he grew up playing and, occasionally, still plays. He has a Nintendo Switch console and there's an online store where you can download classic games. Samus sounds enough like Samson that there will still be continuity—right? Tess should be able to live with that. Or maybe he won't tell her. He finds himself drawn to this notion of a secret name.

It's eighty-six degrees in the house despite the fact that the thermostat has been set to seventy-four all day. So thank goodness here comes the duct guy in his dark blue jumpsuit and steel-toed boots, strutting up the walk.

He lets the guy in. He opens the closet where the crawlspace access is hidden beneath a square of rug. He lifts the exposed panel by a canvas loop and then fixes the loop to a small hook on the back wall of the closet. The guy puts on a headlamp and descends into the hole. Bern sits on the couch. He checks his email, his Twitter, Tess' Instagram, his email again. He texts something sweet to Tess, knowing she is still driving. The guy comes out of the hole. He names a figure. Bern nods. "But the thing," the guy says, "is with all the, you know, this heat, how short-handed we are. So I'll tell 'em this is urgent, because it is urgent, but in all likely we are looking at some weeks, because there are little old ladies from here to Troutdale who we need them to not roast in their kitchenettes."

"Sure," Bern says. "Just give me the first opening you got."

"You'll hear from us," the guy says. He turns to leave—has his hand on the doorknob—but then turns back, having clearly just changed his mind about something. "Is that a Switch?" he says. The video game system sits on the entertainment center next to the TV. He must have noticed it before he first turned toward the door.

"It is," Bern says.

"You play that *Breath of the Wild?*"

"No, I mean not yet."

"I do. I beat it a few times. I beat it and I start again. I love it. I love climbing the volcano and to catch that big horse. I search for herbs and monster parts to make new foods and potions. Hours sometimes, I can do this, like at night after my kid goes down or my day off, you know? I make the colors at the dye works and I do all my outfits. Or I look for korok seeds which, you know, it's the one thing. My best is 580, that's my current game, so there's 320 left to find and I don't even know where they could be. I mean I know this world. I know this whole world. The map shows you where you've been and I've covered every inch. The yellow line of me covering all of it, you know? And the prize for getting them all is just this dumb joke, classic Shigeru Miyamoto joke or maybe it's like a Japanese thing, you know, not him in particular but like *generically* Japanese. Their humor. I don't know if I should say that. But what you win is a little trophy in the game that looks like a poop and it doesn't do anything. No stat boost or open some door. I guess

I'm a completist, but I'm not, I mean not usually. It's more the you know meditative aspect, my wife says spiritual, of the searching, the yellow line of me all over the map—"

"Yeah," Bern says. "I mean I don't know. I haven't, like I said, played it. I like the old games, mostly. You know, the classics?"

"This *is* a classic," the guy says, indignant. "It's the future, the fucking, you know, Shakespeare. But of Nintendo. Do yourself a favor, buddy. Why not see a legend while it's still being made?"

"A legend," Bern says, smirking—barely holding back a laugh—"of Zelda?"

"We'll call you when we have appointments," the guy says, his voice thick with injury. He really leaves this time. Just turns and goes.

Bern locks the door behind him, which he never did lock after Tess left. He goes back to the home office, opens the bottom drawer of the filing cabinet, reaches past old tax returns in hanging folders to the back, where, for two days he has been keeping a bottle of gin that he bought in preparation for Tess being out of town.

She knows he drinks. Indeed, Tess was insistent, when she made her own decision to stop, that he not stop on her account. He can even drink in front of her if he wants to, and if they're at a party or something he often will, but they don't keep alcohol in the house anymore, which Bern is on board with—it was actually his suggestion—but this is a special circumstance. He's going to order a pepperoni pizza, play *Metroid*, drink gin cut with zero-calorie mango-flavor CBD soda until he's too fucked up to play anymore. After that his plan is to jerk off once or (aspirationally) twice to this body-positive OnlyFans he's been into lately, then fall asleep to mild hallucinations abetted by an algorithmically generated playlist of '90s British jungle and EDM.

He's not going to play the original 8-bit *Metroid* from 1986, nor any of the several sequels and reboots from throughout the '00s and '10s (though all of these are available for download via the game's online store) but rather the 16-bit SNES one, the *original sequel*, so to speak, and his favorite: released in 1994, the same year as his Bar Mitzvah, a year before Goldie's monumental debut *Timeless* LP, which he fully expects to hear pieces of on the playlist later, and not that he would've known about 90's British jungle and EDM in 1994 or 95. In those days it was nothing but punk and punk's dorky cousin ska (not that he knew it was dorky yet, not then). He loved Lagwagon, 30FootFall, Skankin' Pickle, Less than Jake—anything that drove his parents crazy, basically, not that that's what he was listening to the music for, but it didn't hurt. He remembers his mother in his bedroom doorway, her head cocked, wearing (no other word for them) Mom Jeans into which were tucked a tee shirt from when she had used to volunteer at the summer day camp he attended; he can picture the pale-yellow fabric with blue text and graphics, the anthropomorphic Star of David grinning and making jazz hands below the clip-art banner that read CAMP KLIPPOT KETANOT 5750 / 1990!!!!, and the bafflement in her voice as sharp as the HVAC guy's indignation just a minute ago when she asked him, "Can they *mean* for it to sound like this?" and how he had replied, without looking up from the game he was playing which may well have been *Metroid* if it wasn't *Street Fighter II: Turbo*, "How should *I* know what *they* meant?"

He can picture her as she is now, too, as she must be, all alone in the big house, three thousand miles and three time zones southeast of here. He should call her, he knows that, but it's already late there. Tomorrow. Tomorrow, he'll call.

Back to his quote unquote bachelor debauch, which by the way Tess would one hundred percent support. She worries he works too much, says he needs to take more time for himself, to learn to unwind and recharge. "Constructive rest," she calls it, another yoga term. The bottom line is that she would in no way begrudge him anything he's going to do this weekend (up to and including the bodpos OFans) and when she comes home on Sunday, or when they check in with each other tomorrow, he'll probably tell her all about it and so none of this is secret, though it somehow enhances the experience to behave for the moment as though it were.

Bern takes the gin to the dining room and puts it on the table. The bottle is clear glass tinted blue and shaped like a tear drop. It's the size of a delicata squash, the gin locally distilled and bottled by a woman-owned company that he can't remember for sure but thinks is also POC friendly or advocative in some way, he thinks the tag said something about something about that, but he threw the tag away when he brought the bottle in the house so to be certain he would have to google it, which he is not about to do. Maybe it's First Nations people the gin supports—that's a big issue out here, people pay more attention to it than they do elsewhere—maybe with a scholarship or internship or profit sharing. Or maybe the tag had just acknowledged that the distillery sits on unceded land.

The flavor profile of this gin, which he has bought before, is frankly rather more floral than he prefers, but he likes to support all the stuff he supports by buying this gin, even if he can't remember what that stuff is right now, and anyway all he's going to taste is the mango-flavored CBD soda. He could have just as easily bought Broker's or Gilbey's or, for that matter, vodka.

He goes to the closet, which is still open, and closes the trap door to the crawlspace. He closes the closet door. He orders the pizza via an app on his phone. He sits down on the couch, picks up the remote to turn on the TV, but then decides he ought to feed Samus before he gets involved in the game. He puts down the remote, goes to the kitchen, gets the can of food out of the fridge and drops it on the counter. Metal on tile is a sound Samus knows. The cat will come bounding in any second, making remarkably good time with his one back leg, which the shelter lady told them had grown extra muscular to compensate. If he had lost one of his front legs, she'd said, that would have permanently screwed up his balance. To lose a back leg had been, in the scheme of things, a stroke of luck.

So okay where is he?

Bern picks up the can and drops it again from a little higher than before.

Nothing.

He's already thinking about the crawlspace, but come on, he was in the room the whole time it was open and he shut it as soon as the guy left—or, well, almost as soon. He went to get the gin, of course, but that took what, thirty seconds. Even if Samus had been curious, he wouldn't have just run over and hopped in. He's probably asleep under their bed, way back against the wall. It's one of his favorite spots in the house and on a day like today also a good place to beat the heat. Bern would crawl back there himself if he thought he could fit.

He heads to the bedroom. Here he is on his belly, almost doing the yoga move called "baby cobra." Up goes the bedskirt: no cat.

The bedroom closet's open so he checks behind the shoe rack that Tess has set up on the floor on her side. On his own side it's a pile of dirty laundry and he can clearly see Samus isn't in it, but he digs through the pile anyway to be sure. To be more sure than sure.

He goes one room at a time: bedroom, bathroom, guest room, office. He opens every drawer and closet, checks under and behind every piece of furniture, even the ones without spaces wide enough to admit his hand, much less a full-grown cat. He jams his eye against every crack and gap.

He checks the windows, confirms that none have been left open. None have. He did this right the first time, earlier, when he turned on the A/C. Waste not, want not. He did everything right. *He did.*

"I did!" he says. Hearing the petulance in his own voice escalates his fear a few degrees. It's rising like heat. He checks the front door to make sure it was properly closed and locked after the duct guy left. It was, as he knew it would be, because he just did it. But what if Tess accidentally left it open? She said it was unlocked, but what if she also hadn't pulled it all the way closed and Samus slipped through it after her, before Bern left the office? But that can't have happened either; he'd remember if he'd found his own front door gaping open. And the cat was still dozing on his desk when he went to greet the duct guy.

He gets the bag of treats out of the pantry, shakes it like a maraca or a grager. Another sound the cat knows well.

"Samus? Samus?"

Continuity, he thinks. His heart is filling with splinters.

"SAMSON!"

Okay. Okay. So it is, must be, however impossibly, the crawlspace. He gets the travel flashlight out of the junk drawer in the kitchen, tests that it works. He lifts and drops the food can once more, just in case, from high enough now that he's worried about cracking the tile on the counter. He goes back to the living room, opens the closet, once again fastens the trap door to the wall by its canvas loop. He gets on his hands and knees with the flashlight in his teeth, stretches his legs and lowers himself slowly with his arms (chaturanga dandasana) until he is flat on the floor, half in and half out of the closet, with his head in the hole. He takes the flashlight out of his mouth and sweeps it across the close, cool, gray-black space: the open grave over which they blithely live their lives.

He can see the rusted-out ducts, the holes at their elbow joints, but if there was a ten-pound animal in one of these flimsy aluminum pipes he'd be able to hear it moving, probably even see the pipe itself move. He points the light at the walls to check the vent screens. There's one with an ominously large rip. So the theory, then, is what? Cat sneaks into the living room while Bern and the guy are talking, or else while Bern is in the office getting the bottle of gin. (Was the cat still in the office when he went back in there? He can't remember. His mind can produce equally vivid images of the office both with and without the cat asleep on the laptop case. He has no idea which is true.) So the cat hops down into the hole and Bern unknowingly shuts him in, but doesn't hear him crying to be let out—or maybe he doesn't cry? Let's say there's a rat, likely the same one that tore the screen to begin with, and when Samus—goddamnit, *Samson*—gives chase it runs up the wall and through the torn screen and he jumps up and follows it (the jump's only three feet, could he manage that? *maybe*) so he winds up in the front yard, at which point he spooks, or maybe is still hunting the rat—or squirrel, it could be a squirrel—and runs off. Goes exploring. Maybe does and maybe doesn't know what a car is, maybe does and maybe doesn't know how to get back to the house, much less inside of it, maybe does and maybe doesn't know that this house is his home.

Bern pulls his head out of the hole, shuts the trap door, shuts the closet, runs back to the kitchen to drop the flashlight and grab the bag of treats. He opens the front door, steps out of the house and directly onto the pizza he ordered. The delivery guy must have left it here when nobody answered the knock, because Bern had paid in-app when he placed the order. He takes the pizza inside and sets it on the table, brushes grit from the caved-in lid of the box. He goes back outside, walks briskly up one side of the block and then the other, shaking the open bag of treats and calling the cat by both his real and his secret name.

Bern sees a cat turn a corner about a block up. The wrong color, but he breaks into a run anyway, makes the turn onto the new street but nothing is there. He probably spooked it. *Idiot.* Three, maybe four blocks down this new street there's an ambulance parked in front of a house. Its siren is off but its lights are on, cherry-red and diamond-white, but pale, so pale in the blazing washout of the cloudless day. Heat lines are rising from the pavement and sweat is pouring down Bern's forehead into his eyes. He stares dumbly at the ambulance, aware of time passing, wasting, but he's frozen, hypnotized by this vision of death. After all, that must be what he's seeing, right? Lights without sound, the EMTs taking their time inside the house because there's nothing left to rush for, nothing to do but clean up the mess and console the family, ease them into their new life with its gaping hole. The way that every moment of every day will be oriented by that absence, how they'll race around its perimeter like dogs at a track. Could have been unexpected, a heart attack, or the bitter relief of a long fight with cancer finally ended, or an old woman roasted like the duct guy said. Could have been a toddler left unattended in a kiddie pool. *I just went in to grab my phone,* the anguished father cries, *I wanted to take a picture of her playing to send to her mom.* Bern, back when he thought he was going to be a father, always feared he would do something boneheaded like that: a tiny lapse in judgment, unretractable, shearing apart the family like lightning cleaves a tree.

And how else to describe the current debacle but as his deep fear finally realized, his nightmare come true?

You never said Kaddish.

The voice is his father's, and that's only one of several reasons why this thought is insane. Tess isn't Jewish and Bern doesn't practice, so there's that. Neither did Bern's parents when he was growing up. The Bar Mitzvah, well he did that, sure, but that was just this…thing that happened. He isn't a member of a synagogue, doesn't even know if there are any in Portland, though he assumes there must be a few. Obviously, he and Tess are not people who would believe that life begins at conception. The pregnancies they lost were lost potential, not *dead children.* And yet he thinks—or rather, he hears—the insane sentence a second time.

You never said Kaddish.

It occurs to Bern that his father must be talking about himself.

He feels the preheat of tears behind his eyes (such a different heat than the heat of the heatwave) and decides that if he's going to lose his mind, he should text Tess about Samson before he does. He scatters a few treats on the ground, an offering to the vanished stray, turns away from the ambulance, walks toward home where his phone will be right where he left it on the couch cushion where he put it down after he ordered the pizza.

She's going to leave you.

Not his father's voice now but his own.

His own voice speaking the words now, and later again, with pronouns and tenses shifted—*she left me*—when he will have to tell his mother; the flash that will pass through her eyes right before her whole expression shatters: he can see it, how it will be, though they'll be on the phone, not Zoom or FaceTime, when he tells her (she used to sat jokingly say that she would not bother to learn how to video chat until there was a grandbaby to wave at; she no longer makes the joke, but still hasn't learned) and she'll be standing at the side table where the cordless phone was sitting in its charging cradle before she picked it up, the empty cradle blinking blue (blue as his gin bottle) in the foyer of her big empty house where she raised a family and lost her husband and now lives alone, knowing she ought to sell while the market is hot, get something right-sized, a condo or independent living place, somewhere there'd be people around to talk to, or to call if she ever needs help. Maybe he'll move back in if she suggests it, at least for a while. They'll never say who was doing who the favor, or even what exactly the favor was.

He opens the front door to his house and steps inside and here is Samson on the dining room table, swatting at the delivery box. The bouquet of hot cheese fills the house.

Bern will discover Samson's hiding place tomorrow. He'll be reaching for a pair of pants on the high shelf in the bedroom closet. It's a six-foot leap, higher than he'd have ever imagined that a cat, much less a three-legged cat, could jump. He himself can't even see up there, he just reaches for whatever pair is on top of the pile. That's why he didn't think to check. What can he say? He didn't know. But here are his good gray slacks coated in a layer of orange fur. It'll be another few days before he'll catch Samson in the act of leaping up there, and another week before he manages to film said leap on his phone. He will forward the video to Tess, who will post it to her Instagram, where it will unexpectedly go viral. Five days and eighty-seven thousand likes later, Tess, Bern, and Samson will be the subject of a short feel-good video segment on the website of the local newspaper. Samson's original owner will see the segment, wrongly assume that the cat is now very valuable, some kind of reality star, and convince himself that he was tricked into giving it up. He will attempt to sue the animal shelter, and after that fails, he will show up at Tess's yoga studio, hollering about what he's owed. Tess will have to stop class and call the police. She will feel sympathy for this pathetic and deluded person, but at Bern's insistence will, reluctantly, take out a restraining order. Two weeks later, right when it will seem as though the drama is over and things are back to normal, she'll fall off the wagon. Bern will have to pick her up from a bar on the other side of town, near the apartment they lived in before they bought the house. Bern will worry that this is a full-on relapse, but it won't be. She'll give up her chip and start over. By the time she re-earns the three year chip she will be seven months pregnant with their daughter, who will be born healthy but will turn out to be allergic to cats. Tess will suggest to Bern, jokingly, that they look up the former owner to see if he'd still be interested in having Samson back. They'll have a laugh over this, but it will be sad laughter, and they'll wish they hadn't. Later that night, after Tess and the baby are both sleeping, Bern will look up the former owner, curious whatever happened to him, and it will turn out that he died a year earlier, a suicide, though the obituary won't quite spell this out. Bern, for a moment, will see the silent ambulance brightly shining at the end of the sweltering street, like a light at the end of a tunnel that is also made of light. Ever since that day Samson went missing, Bern has associated this image with the horror of loss and the miracle of restoration, which is to say with the mystery of being and the grace of God, though of course he would never, will never, say this *to* anyone, or even articulate it in these terms to himself. It's a knowledge beyond knowing, or perhaps beneath it, a secret untellable because it isn't made of language, and even if you could name it, you would never speak the name. And he never does say kaddish for his father, though his wife and daughter will, eventually, at the daughter's insistence, say kaddish for him.

But right now all Bern knows is that Samson is here, that he was in the house this whole time, and that Tess isn't going to leave him. He tries to comprehend the scale of the disaster he has been spared—the vast, hauntological void of its non-incarnation—and all he can think of is that article about the earthquake and the tsunami, the one that Tess kept talking about last summer. He lets his legs weaken and bend, a controlled collapse into child's pose, sobbing, his forehead to the hardwood floor, not thinking at all of the lost pregnancies—not even for a second—as the cat, having given up on the impenetrable pizza box, hops down from the table and sets himself between Bern's outstretched arms. Samson sits waiting on his single haunch, and so when Bern lifts his face from the earth he finds himself eye to eye with the cat, who now—and only now—begins to purr and nuzzle him, to extend an exploratory paw (with claws retracted) to the side of Bern's damp face. *Little mittens, like the nursery rhyme.* He can see himself reflected in those eyes, twinned in fact, a tiny brace of Berns like flies trapped in amber, only not amber and not trapped. Maybe game sprites then, explorers lost in the foreign gold-flecked green worlds of iris, and that green in retreat as Samson's pupils go from slits to ovals with the warm black of want, and nothing is lost, least of all Bern, who sees himself adrift in that dilating darkness and allows it to welcome him home.

The Cactus' Novel

Evan Williams

The cactus goes on a road trip and, while traveling, gets an idea for a novel. He stops at a diner and orders breakfast. While he waits with his coffee he takes from his body a single spine. With its sharpest point, the cactus scratches the opening lines of his novel into the diner table. His food comes, and he eats slowly. He does not eat the yolk of his last fried egg. Instead, with the spine's sharpest point, he pricks it, tilting his plate to let the yellow slide into the scratches he'd made earlier. In this way, the opening lines to the cactus' novel sparkle alertly on the diner table. He pays his tab and leaves the story.

The Lifers

Emily Nelson

When his wife shoots the neighbor's sheep he thinks *alright, I guess there's something wrong*. Up to this point, he's noticed a few new strange behaviors here and there, a husband's instinct that the woman beside him is not exactly the same woman that he was sitting next to a few moments ago. Occasionally he catches a cloudy look in Denise's eye that he has never seen before, confusion that reads like fear, but there will always be a blink and she returns. He is able to tell himself, after these moments pass, that she's just slowing down a bit, like they all are at this age. Even when she is cruel to him out of the blue, or when she goes for a walk and forgets the way home—all things that he can explain away, however desperately. Those things that happen as you age. Killing the neighbor's sheep is not one of those things.

"They were on our property" is the excuse she gives him when he arrives home to find her shivering on the couch in her bathrobe, away from the crowd of people who have gathered out front to witness the spectacle of bloodied wool and sheep brains on the lawn. Tate did not see it happen, but there are several witnesses; Tilden Island is small enough that despite the acres between neighbors, not much goes unnoticed, especially when a gunshot rattles everyone at seven in the morning outside of hunting season. When Tate had left the house that morning, Denise had been sitting at the kitchen table drinking coffee and doing the crossword puzzle on her iPad as she always did. He had not worried about leaving her alone.

Sam had been the first one there, had just happened to be driving down to the dock when he saw Denise standing on her porch with Tate's shotgun in her hands, the heaving carcasses of three Merino sheep in the front yard. Sam told Tate that Denise was crying when he found her, and for a moment she seemed so disoriented, he wasn't sure if she was going to turn the gun on him next. But when Sam reached for the shotgun, she gave it to him wordlessly, her hands limp, before retreating into the house and locking the door behind her.

The sheep belonged to Grace Pham, who lived on the other side of the island, and it wasn't clear what they were doing so far from home. One of them died outright, and the other two were wounded so badly by the buckshot that Sam had to finish them off before Grace was even notified. Nobody wanted Grace to call the police, but she did anyway. There is no law enforcement on Tilden Island, one of the many reasons that Tate and the other lifers love living here. The homeowner's association voted against building a sheriff's outpost on the island a few years back, citing concerns about land availability that were really just flimsy cover for the usual libertarian worries about government overreach. Most of the lifers are here precisely *because* there was no law enforcement, and while there has never been anything more serious than a speeding violation in the last twenty years, it has been understood by everyone that the police very rarely need to get involved, that everyone on Tilden can work things out like grownups.

Obviously Grace feels differently. She's much younger than Tate, probably not even out of her forties, and has not been on the island as long as him. She wears expensive leggings and college sweatshirts, and has clean hands for someone who works with sheep so much. One of the few people Tate doesn't know all that well, one of the few people on the island that hasn't had dinner at the Waylan's, never received a can of Denise's cherry plum preserves. Not out of spite, of course. Grace keeps to herself more than most, out there on the rich side of the island with the tourists and part-time residents. Her standing in his yard makes Tate feel uncomfortable, something that was never supposed to happen.

The police take a report from Grace over the phone and tell her that they will be in touch. Denise could be charged with "maliciously killing or causing substantial bodily harm to livestock belonging to another," a Class C felony with a ten-thousand dollar fine or up to five years in prison, depending on the findings of the judge. He expects Grace to be hysterical, crying like Denise did over the loss of her animals, but instead she is maddeningly quiet, her eyes sympathetic as she talks over the situation with Sam. When Mitch Jackson finally arrives with his pickup to take the carcasses to his burn pile, Grace turns to Tate and presses her lips together.

"I'm really sorry about this, Tate," she says, her voice heavy with a familiarity that the two of them do not share. "I'm sorry this is happening to you and Denise."

She climbs into her golf cart and speeds down the dirt road towards her side of the island, following Mitch's pickup. Sam lets out a sigh through his teeth.

"This is bad," he says, and it's so obvious of an observation that Tate almost laughs.

He finds Denise in the living room. She's changed out of her robe and is watching the television on mute. The San Juan County news is playing, a shiny-haired woman gesturing broadly at kitschy graphics of the sun and rain clouds. He has barely had a second alone with her all morning.

"Gonna be nice this week," Denise says. She smiles up at Tate, her glasses sliding down her nose.

"Denise," he starts, but she's already looking past him and suddenly stands up.

"I'm making lunch," she says, sweeping into the kitchen. He watches her go, every limb weighing a thousand pounds. She doesn't seem to realize what has happened. The woman on television is now gesticulating towards a cluttered traffic pattern, her eyes sparkling in HD.

"Denise, honey," he says again.

"I'm in here, Tate," she calls. "I can't hear you." He gets as far as the kitchen doorway, watching her rifle through the cupboards. She's murmuring to herself, her voice low and undulating, almost as if she's singing.

"I was just thinking that we need to start planning our Christmas cards this year," Denise says, turning and smiling at Tate. "I always feel like we get behind on it and then we're rushing to do it at the last minute. Don't you think?"

"Denise, honey, it's August." Tate watches her go through the knife drawer, and wonders briefly if he should hide those too. He's familiar with the pattern of her days; if she starts out lucid, she will generally stay that way, but the earlier the incident comes, the longer she stays disoriented.

"Well, I know, but…" Denise procures the bread knife and starts hacking at the half-stale loaf of sourdough on the counter. "I wanted to do a newsletter this year. Lots of people do them, and I think it would be nice. Something to let our friends know what's going on with our lives. What we've been up to and everything."

"What have we been doing?" Tate asks. He hopes it doesn't sound like a challenge.

Denise turns to him again. "Lots of things, silly," she says, smiling. "We rebuilt the Bearcat in April, and I've got the new herb garden set up. You're the secretary for the Homeowner's Association. People want to know what we're up to."

She goes back to her work. It seems foolish for

him to point out that they haven't sent out Christmas cards for at least ten years; they don't have anyone to keep in touch with on the mainland, and everyone on Tilden already knows everything about everybody.

"Honey," he says, "I talked to Sam Sparrow just now."

"About what?" Denise does not turn around.

"I—about what happened this morning."

"Oh, that," Denise says, and she turns slightly to pull a bowl from the sink. He tries to catch her facial expression, but the sun burning off the fog outside is reflecting in her glasses. Her mouth is firm, unreadable.

"He says that they'll need to confiscate our guns. And that there will be some sort of fine." Tate watches his wife's back move up and down beneath her denim shirt as she scoops celery and onions into the bowl. She doesn't turn around.

"Well, I think we'll be alright," is all she says.

"Honey, they're going to take all our guns," he says, feeling slightly desperate. "Grace wants to take legal action."

Denise waves her knife-wielding hand dismissively. "Oh, she's just uptight. She'll relax. It's not like she doesn't have eighty more sheep where those ones come from."

Tate thinks, *well, at least she knows what she did.*

"You shouldn't say that, Denise," Tate hears himself saying. "This isn't a joke. She did say she wanted to sue us."

"She'll cool off," Denise says. Then, "I'm making chicken salad, do you want some?"

Tate rakes a hand through his hair. It feels greasy and damp, as if he has run several miles, even though he has been standing still for what feels like hours now.

"No, honey. You know I don't like it."

He sees her stiffen before turning around and nodding.

"Of course," she says. "I just wanted to make sure."

"Anyways," Tate tries again. "Sam was telling me what we're going to have to do next. With the trial and all."

Denise freezes. "Trial?"

"For the felony," Tate says, almost afraid. "The felony charge. For shooting Grace's—"

Denise drops the knife and whirls around.

"Did that bitch really call the cops on me?" The look on her face is more betrayal than anger. "Just because of that?"

Tate feels defensive, pulling away from the doorframe. He has a sudden desire to hide from his wife, a feeling he has never had and never wants to have again.

"Honey, it's…" he looks at the floor. "It's technically a crime, what you did. I can't—"

"I'm gonna call her," Denise says, darting past Tate towards the landline in the living room. Tate races after her.

"No, Denise," he says, catching her and wrestling the receiver from her hand. "It's already done. If you call her it's only going to make it worse."

Her hand is wrapped around his wrist, her frail fingernails biting the skin of his arm. Up close, her eyes are wet, pleading.

"It's not my fault," she says. "They were on our property. What was I supposed to do?"

When they met, they were both divorcees, her three years out and him only six months. They met on a flight from Seattle to Sacramento; she was a flight attendant, and he swore to himself he wouldn't do anything funny, make any moves like he had seen his father do when he was a little kid. He only asked her out when he ran into her at the arrival deck, both of them trying to get a cab, and he decided it must be fate to see her again. She had changed her shoes and was wearing glossy white sneakers instead of pumps, and her hair was falling out of its twist. Denise said that she had gotten left behind in the bathroom and missed the crew bus; years later, he would know that this was a lie, that she had stopped for a drink at the airport bar without telling the rest of the flight crew. They got to talking and agreed to split a cab, first dropping her off at her hotel and then him at his. But when they arrived at the Sacramento Sheraton, Denise invited Tate in to get a drink at the hotel bar, and he obliged.

He loved how easy she was to talk to, not a hint of insecurity. She was a woman who had seen the world and was largely unimpressed with its inhabitants, but those who surpassed her expectations she loved with a ferocity that reminded Tate of a mother lion. Neither of them had any children, him by accident and her by choice, one of the many reasons she and her first husband didn't work out. When he left the bar that evening, she followed him out, the two of them bathed in the fungal orange light of the streetlamps. They stood for a moment, letting the cool wind scatter the leaves across the parking lot.

"How long are you here for?" she finally asked. Her four vodka sodas had turned her cheeks pink, and even though she was well into her fifties she looked like a young woman.

"Oh, just a few days. I'm in town for a meeting, but then I'm going back to Seattle."

"Well..." she adjusted her coat, cheap polyester standard-issued from the airline she worked for. "Give me a call the next time you're in town. I'd love to do this again."

He wrote his number for her on a piece of hotel stationary, and she took it. She moved like she was going to hug him, then reached out and patting his upper arm.

When he got home a few days later, the light on his voicemail machine was blinking. It was Denise, asking him to get drinks again sometime soon. A year later, they were married.

#

The officers from the county are at their house a week after the "incident," as Sam Sparrow has delicately begun to call it. Tate watches them from the upstairs window as they pull up on someone's borrowed ATV: soft, middle-aged men with round pink faces and dark glasses. One of them has a beard, red streaked with gray, and neither wears a uniform. He expected something different when he was told that men from the state government would be coming to remove all the guns from the premises; in his head, he envisioned a swarm of stiff-backed g-men in tactical gear descending on the airstrip, ready for a fight. Even if this were the case, Tate is not going to fight; in another circumstance, certainly. But the man from the county explained it over the phone to him that morning.

"It's a precautionary measure, ahead of any potential fines," he'd said. Tate was only half listening, watching Denise in the living room look at the television impassively. "We'll have to take all firearms out of the house until Mrs. Waylan is deemed psychologically sound." Tate appreciated that the man said "until," as if this stranger was also sure that there was nothing really wrong with Denise deep down, that this was all a temporary arrangement, and that eventually everything would clear and they could go back to their normal life.

He meets the officers in his front yard, hoping to keep them away from Denise, who does not know that any of this is happening. The officers show Tate their badges, introduce themselves as Officer Beasly and Officer Smith. Both of them are young enough to be Tate's own children.

"Can you tell us how many guns you have on the property, sir?" the smaller one, Officer Smith, asks. Neither of them have taken off their sunglasses and Tate sees himself reflected through them, his face swollen and helpless in their eyes.

Tate shrugs before he can realize that he shouldn't. It looks careless, the attitude of someone who doesn't keep track of his firearms, the type of person who would let his rapidly deteriorating wife destroy someone else's property without thinking twice.

"Twenty-five," Tate says finally. The taller one, Beasly, writes something down on his notepad.

"And you have them all out of their safes? Unlocked?"

"Yes." What is unsaid is that they were not in the safe to begin with. It was Denise who convinced him that a gun safe was necessary in the first place, and while he had gotten one shipped over from Anacortes a few years back, it had gone unused and the guns stayed unloaded in his office. Denise had said more than once that she didn't think he needed so many—after all, the biggest threat on Tilden was Anton Check's old Charolais bull, Timothy—but she agreed that it was his right and as long as she didn't have to trip over them, he could have as many as he wanted.

He follows the officers into the house, watching from the doorway as they loaded the guns into containers. They sweep the house, Tate trying to keep them as far from the living room as possible without it looking suspicious. They tell Tate that they will be in touch if anything changes and give him a phone number for the SJPD if he has any questions before buzzing down the road back towards the dock. Tate watches them leave. A small crowd, noticing the officers when they arrived, are gathered outside the Waylan property to watch the proceedings. Sam Sparrow is there, and when the ATV rounds the bend towards the dock he makes a motion to the onlookers and they head on their way. Sam gives Tate a sympathetic look, shakes his head. "Doesn't he have anything better to do?" Tate mutters to himself.

Denise has been in the living room for all of this. She's finally turned off the television and is reading a magazine when Tate returns.

"Why were the police here?" Denise asks, not looking up from the page.

#

It shocked him at that age that love could still feel this way, giddy and bashful. It was different with her, different than he expected marriage or love to be now that he was closer to retirement than starting life. The wedding hadn't been big, a courthouse affair on a Tuesday morning, Tate in the suit he wore for business meetings and Denise in a pale blue skirt-set, a bouquet of roses from the grocery store across the street. She moved into his house out by the Boeing plant in Everett and settled into a life quickly, the two of them almost dangerously happy. She had a mission to protect people: waitresses at their local diner, the mail carrier, her dry cleaner, taking it upon herself to take care of them, tipping too much and bringing them clothes she was going to donate. Even when her hairdresser massacred her dye job, Denise insisted on going back the next time she needed her hair done. "If she loses customers, she'll get kicked out of the salon," was her logic. "She's got three kids at home and no husband, what am I supposed to do?"

When he learned that she had been hiding his

drinking from him, he was more humiliated by the fact that he had not noticed anything sooner, that she had been able to keep it from him so easily. She had been a functioning alcoholic for several years, and by the time Tate entered her life she was an expert. But her tenacity for deceit was slipping in old age, and ultimately the catalyst was being drunk on the job, which led to her being fired from Horizon, hauled off the plane sobbing in Portland. She was four years away from her pension when it happened, but Tate assured her they made more than enough without it.

The move to Tilden came later, not long after Denise got out of rehab. All of Tate's friends from work were moving out of Seattle, looking for smaller towns or states with less rain and crime and liberalism, and it was one of these men who told Tate about Tilden, intrigued him with the idea of an "off the grid" place to live out his golden years. Tilden wasn't connected to the ferry route like most of the other islands north of Puget Sound. There was no law enforcement presence on the island, nor any stores or restaurants; there wasn't enough need or want for anything like it. It sounded like a paradise to Tate and Denise, both of whom were getting increasingly desperate to leave Seattle for different reasons, and when they went to visit one summer before Tate retired they fell in love.

They arrived in April, snatching up a prime piece of property by the airport that was really a glorified landing strip near the mail shed. The house was two stories, a rarity on Tilden, with a big wraparound porch on the second floor with a view of the Salish sea out the dining room window. At first, Tate had been worried that the change in lifestyle would be too much for both of them, but Denise took to it immediately. She had never been a woman much concerned with her appearance, but on Tilden she quickly adopted the uniform of the other retired wives, trading slacks and sweaters for loose denim shirts and practical work pants, letting her hair go gray and coarse instead of heat styling it every day. There was a garage where Tate and Denise worked on their airplane, a Cessna 206 they bought secondhand from a fellow islander and repaired as one of their first retirement projects. Denise built a garden like the one she had at home in Everett, stringing up netting around the plot to keep deer and rabbits at bay. Both of them read every day, worked on projects—he wanted to build airplanes, so she helped, and she wanted to grow more food, so he dug her a garden. They didn't install a TV for almost three years after moving in. On warm evenings they sat on the porch and watched the bats chase after mosquitos as night closed in, the only noise the occasional call of an owl or the dull roar of a neighbor's ATV, the plaintive cry of a foghorn somewhere on the water. She even gave up smoking, the only vice she had kept after rehab.

"It just feels wrong to do it here," she said. "Everywhere I look there's trees and grass and I can't stop thinking about accidentally setting it on fire." She told Tate how surprised she was about how easy it was to quit, something she had never been able to do on the mainland. "Island magic," she called it.

They settled into a routine that, to Tate, was

nothing short of idyllic, and every morning when he rolled over to find Denise already out of bed, dressed and working in the garden before it got too warm or too rainy, he would see her reading glasses balanced haphazardly on the nightstand and feel a rush of calm that he had, up to that point, only ever associated with coming home after a long day of work.

Early on, Tate had wondered what would happen if he or Denise got sick. At the time, it wasn't likely; they went to their doctor's appointments on the mainland every year, got checked for everything. Tate's family was unusually healthy, and his own mother had lived to ninety-nine before dying peacefully of old age. Denise was not close with her family, and had not been for some time, so she didn't know if there were any health issues to be aware of. But they were both in good health—you had to be, to weather the cold winters and long boat rides and hours spent working in the sun that came with life on Tilden. Tate never worried, and the two of them had already planned where they would like to be buried together on the island.

When someone on Tilden got sick, really sick, they moved off-island to deal with it. A faceless realtor whom nobody had ever seen would sell their house, and it would be like that old sick person had never been there. There were no wailing sirens to cut through the night, no sudden heart attacks or strokes. Like most things on Tilden Island, death usually came at a leisurely pace, always with enough time for one to prepare for its approach. Enough time to get your affairs in order, enough time to vanish off the island before anyone saw you sick or weak or broken, had to think of the fate that was no doubt awaiting all of them. There had never been an on-island funeral, unless you count the wake that the McIvers held for their 16-year-old cat, Katrina, after she died of kidney failure.

A lot of the homeowners only stayed for the spring and summer, taking their old bones to warmer climes for the harsher part of the year. Over the years, Tate saw several long-time neighbors move, gathering the castoffs they left behind as they returned to the security and confinement of the mainland. It was how Tate got his truck, the fishing boat, a trailer and more buoys than he knew what to do with. The collection grew with time: Denise strung the buoys across the deck like enormous year-round Christmas lights, Tate put the stag horns from Andy Wood on the grill of his truck. A colorful array of paintings, photographs, and maps from past residents lined the walls of the Waylan home, and there was even a dog at one time, an aging Golden Retriever named Buddy who was too old to manage the boat ride and was now buried in Tate and Denise's backyard near the garden.

"I'll stay as long as I'm able. You'll have to drag me off kicking and screaming," Denise always said, and Tate believed her. He kept waiting for something, a lump or a twinge or a sudden loss of appetite to signal that their time was coming, and for years it never came. Tate and Denise began to watch neighbors their age deteriorate and move away, selling their houses or going part-time, and without meaning to they became the longest-standing residents of Tilden Island.

Sam calls again later that evening. Tate wishes he wouldn't; Sam is only trying to help, he takes his job as the HOA director very seriously—perhaps too seriously—but it's almost more than he can take after today.

"We're doing fine, Sam," Tate says before he can say anything.

"I know, Tate. I just wanted to let you know that Grace decided that she is gonna go through with it after all and take it to court if you don't pay the fine."

Tate glances at Denise, who is cleaning the dishes at the sink, and turns his body away from her.

"The ten thousand?"

"Yeah."

"Why doesn't she tell me that?" Tate asks.

"She will. I told her to call you. But I wanted to give you a heads up."

Tate rubs his eyes behind his glasses. "So that's it? She wants the fine and everything?"

"Yeah. She says she's really sorry about it, but it's a loss of inventory, so she feels like—"

"Bullshit," Tate says. "If she was really that sorry she wouldn't have dragged the police into it. She wouldn't have made it such a big deal."

"I hear you," Sam says carefully. "But I guess she feels it's what she has to do."

"She didn't have to do anything. Can't she tell it was an accident?"

A pause. "Well, I mean…." Sam sighs. "I know,

but to be fair to Grace it didn't really look like an accident. But listen, Tate, I tried to talk her down, and I think she's listening. I told her—I mean, we all know that Denise hasn't been doing so good lately."

This is a surprise to Tate. He thought he was the only one who had noticed the changes in his wife's behavior, at least until now. Shame floods him; what has Denise done or said to Sam that would make him realize that she's not as sharp as she used to be?

"What do you mean?" Tate asks. Denise is murmuring to herself again, the low thrumming words that sound like singing.

"Come on, you know how it is with old age. Dementia and all that, makes you act different. I'm sure if you told the judge that, they'd be more lenient with you. Maybe even let you settle. But I don't know, I'm not a legal expert or anything."

"Yeah," Tate says, because what else can he say?

"Listen, a bunch of us are gonna help you out. Nobody wants to see you guys go through something like this. I've got Greta working on a list of all the folks who can bring you guys food, Annette was talking about helping out with the house—"

"Sam," Tate says, harsher than he means to. "Nobody's dead. You don't need to do that."

"I know, but—"

"If you can get me ten thousand dollars, I'd sure appreciate it. Or a time machine. Other than that, we don't need anything."

He can't tell who hangs up first. All the phone calls are starting to make him feel unfaithful somehow, a secret that everyone is in on except for Denise.

Tate thinks about what Sam said, imagines trying to explain to Denise what their options are now, ask her if she understands what is happening and what it might mean for the two of them. He sees hospitals, retirement homes, dust-colored hallways and waiting rooms reeking of other people's breath. Sedate watercolors on the walls, IV drips, handfuls of pills that Denise won't swallow because she's never liked swallowing pills, even Advil has to get crushed up in her orange juice. A quiet life of crossword puzzles and dinner on the deck turned into a series of appointments, in-home care, constant boats back and forth to the mainland, the faceless realtor materializing to tell Tate what the house might be worth.

"Honey?" Denise startles Tate from his vision. She's finished the dishes and is wiping her hands with the sunflower towel, a castoff from the retired schoolteacher who moved to Alaska.

"What are you thinking about?" she asks. Tate shakes his head.

"Nothing, honey," he says, and she comes up behind him and squeezes his shoulders. He feels her forehead come to rest between his shoulder blades.

"It's getting late, my love," she says. The closest Denise usually gets to pet names is "honey," and the intensity of the words catch Tate off guard. Her arms snake around his chest and clasp tight.

"I know. We should get to bed."

Tate can't fall asleep, but at some point he must drop off, because one moment he's staring at the ceiling and the next moment he is on his stomach and Denise's side of the bed is empty. He jolts up immediately, fumbling in the dark for his glasses. There is no sound from the house, just the endless whirr of crickets drifting through the windows. The fan shut off sometime during the night, and Tate's shirt is plastered to his front with sweat.

"Denise?" He called down the hallway, but there was no answer. Panic seizes him; there are no more guns in the house, but God knows what Denise could find to wreak havoc with. He bolts down the hall and is relieved to see the keys on their usual hook. At least she hasn't taken the car anywhere.

He calls her name again. If she's gone out on foot, it wouldn't be much better. It's three in the morning, she won't know the way back. Even with the clearest of memories, Tilden Island is incredibly dark at night. No lights from streets or buildings—one of the many blessings of living so far away from civilization.

When he goes out on the porch and looks into the yard he sees her, bending down in her garden, surrounded by the late-summer harvest that is caged in to keep out the deer and rabbits. She was still wearing her robe, the same blue terry cloth one she wore that first night she slept over at his house in Everett. Under the glow of the quarter moon he watches her work, her fingers moving gently through the dirt, harvesting or weeding or watering, he can't see. A cold wind moves across the lawn; autumn is on its way. Denise is not worried.

my cowboy

Harriet Prebble

I lead him to the bed
in the choke cold of dawn,
spurs skimming the hardwood floor,
steam rising off our flesh like fire.
Push down his bound shoulders,
linger on the sweat-soaked cotton,
press my lips against his bristles,
slipping his wide-brim hat
off his perennially furrowed brow.

Slide a hand onto his heart,
grasp it, pulsing wet and firm,
pry the weapon from his grip
and release.
Clean the blood from him,
pick the dirt off his bones,
hold his slick head against my chest,
hum a lullaby
into his skull.

Take him in my mouth,
sink my nails into his thighs,
drink in the rolling rumbles,
spit out his weak will,
catch him as he falls,
then fold him into pressed linen.
Stand a moment, peering down,
consider absolution, but relent
and close the door behind me.

Grip the porcelain of the washhouse sink,
brace myself, and pick the metal from my gut.
Dig down into the dirt
outside the old porch, leaking.
Nail a cross at the head of the hole
and climb in.
Lay back and let the cold air enter me,
see the mountains for the first time,
see the rolling clouds anew.

No Man's Land

Mike Nagel

J says I'm talking in my sleep again. It happens a couple times a year. Some worm hole opens up to my subconscious between one and two AM.

"Anything interesting?" I say.

"Not really," she says.

I heard a mattress ad on a podcast the other day that said we spend one-third of our lives asleep but failed to address what seemed to me the real issue here which is what to do about the two-thirds of our lives that we spend awake, just sort of walking around.

"What are you up to these days," Matt asks over coffee.

"Same as you," I say. "Trying not to be a total joke."

Yesterday was my thirty-fifth birthday. The beginning of my thirty-sixth year. By 9am it was ninety-two degrees outside. By 10am it was a hundred and three. Around noon I saw on Twitter that the Supreme Court had reversed Roe v. Wade. 5 to 4.

Well, I think. It's not like we didn't see it coming.

Nothing surprising has ever happened in the entire history of the world. If you're surprised by something, you just didn't have enough information is all.

Now that I'm halfway through my thirties—conservatively speaking: halfway through my life—here at the mid-point of this amateur musical-theater production of my existence, I'm faced with the very real possibility that I've already gotten the gist. That I more or less get what's going on here. That there's nothing left to do but play dumb and make art and try to act surprised when everything that I know is going to happen eventually happens.

Try, I mean, to appreciate all of this for what it is.

This is our second summer in this house on Majestic Drive. Down the street from Bob Woodruff park. Not far from the Bowman Russel Cemetery where all those dead Bowmans and Russels are buried. Where at least one Bowman-Russel is buried. The final resting place of Sarah E. Gamble Chenault, whoever that was. Probably somebody who thought they were important. We like it here okay. It's friendly and smells like hot dogs. It's middle class, middle brow, smack in the middle of Middle America.

Everyone drives a pre-owned Honda Accord and weedwacks constantly. Two or three times a week. All day on Saturday. At any given time, on any given day, somebody in our neighborhood is engaged in some form of landscaping. I read in Scientific American that America's most-grown crop is the front lawn.

In Be Brief and Tell Them Everything, Brad Listi worries that we're living in a uniquely stupid time in history. But I find that idea more hopeful than the more-likely scenario which is that it's been exactly this stupid the whole way through. There is no difference, Earnest Becker says, between us and anybody else who's ever lived. The Psychic Unity of Mankind. All human beings throughout history are 100% interchangeable. "Standard vintage Homo Sapiens," he calls us. Just a bunch of schmoes.

For my thirty-fifth birthday dinner we order kids meals off the Pepper Pals® kids' menu from Chili's To Go. Half the food for half the price. J gets the Pepper Pals® Cheesy Chicken Pasta. I get the Pepper Pals® Crispy Crispers. We share a mini Chocolate Molten cake. It costs like twenty bucks. Tip included.

While we sit there in the parking lot waiting for our food, I notice the thermometer on J's dashboard. Two hundred and twenty-three degrees, it says. Then it says: two hundred and twenty-four. Really getting up there. Going for the record. When it hits two hundred and twenty five I ask J how she feels about the whole Supreme Court abortion thing. That's what I call it. "The whole supreme court abortion thing."

"I haven't quite decided how I feel about it yet," J says.

"A feeling isn't something you decide," I say. "A feeling is something you feel."

"Okay," she says. "Then I haven't quite felt the way I feel about it yet. Happy?"

Sometimes I worry that we're not upset enough about the right things. That our chilled-out middle-class detachment is less a sign of enlightenment than proof that we're just not very good people. Yeats said that thing about the best lacking all conviction. The best people I know are all fucking pissed.

"I feel like we should be more worked up about it," I say.

"Yeah," J says. "Maybe."

Later we watch Mission Impossible IV: Ghost Protocol. Like every Mission Impossible movie, this one's all about teamwork. My friend Matt, a screenwriter out in LA, says every movie is a battle between ideas. Teamwork vs. Self-Sufficiency. Family vs. Country. Friendship vs. Justice. The best movies are never Good vs. Evil. They're always Good vs. Good. It reminds me of Vonnegut, how he said he'd never written a villain. It's disturbing to think there might not be any.

The real enemy, Earnest Becker reminds us in Escape from Evil, is always within.

Saturday afternoon the temperature in Plano hits a hundred and four. According to the thermometer in J's Jeep: three hundred and ninety-eight. The hottest summer in recent memory. Every summer in Texas is the hottest summer in recent memory. Recent memory is fifteen seconds long. After that you've gone LONG TERM, somewhere outside the hippocampus, deep inside no man's land, a notoriously unreliable place to get your information. Not that I know anything about how brains work, of course. I know they're made of old sponges and alphabet soup. And I know they're pretty fucked up. Up in Purgatory, Pete told me that our brains and stomachs are more closely connected than most people realize. He'd read an article about it in Prevention Magazine. Gut health is mental health. It is possible to poop your way to a whole new you. Pete once took a shit so massive it cured his depression.

"True story," he said.

I think if I were happier with my life I might be a little more upset about it being halfway over. As it is I'm more or less fine with it. Not too worked up. It's not like it's a surprise or anything. The other day I saw a picture of a man from 1878, just standing there in the middle of some house in Plano with his hands at his sides, having no idea he was already dead.

Look at this schmoe I thought.

At a dinner party Sunday night, our friend Molly makes gluten-free lasagna and low-sodium Caesar salad. She puts red grapes in one bowl and green grapes in a different bowl. A cutting board with apple slices and sharp cheddar cheese. We drink lime-flavored Topo Chico and A&W Cream Soda. Some of us aren't drinking alcohol on purpose. Some of us just happen to not be drinking alcohol. That about sums up the alcohol situation at this point in my life. Abstinence with varying degrees of intentionality. As an appetizer, Molly serves CVS-brand acid-reducers and tropical flavored Tums.

"Now that we're all middle aged," she says, going around the table, tapping them out of their bottles and into our hands. Not that I need any help remembering. Recently my cousin texted me the results of her latest colonoscopy. It seems the doctors didn't like what they found up there.

"Well what did they think they were going to find up there?" I said. "Something likeable?"

It's possible our expectations for what we'll find up our butts might be a tad high.

"What I'm trying to tell you," my cousin said, "is that it might be a good idea to should schedule yours sooner rather than later."

"And what I'm trying to tell you," I said, "is that there is a big difference between what people tell me and what I choose to hear."

Recent news items: Jan. 6 committee to hear bombshell testimony from Trump insider; Pregnant woman ticketed in HOV lane claims fetus was her passenger; Texans urged to conserve power as extreme heatwave strains power grid; "I thought there would be more outcry," Highland Park shooting victim says.

When I was a kid I believed the world was six thousand years old and due to end any day now. Now I believe the world is five billion years old and due to end any day now.

This morning I got a weather alert on my phone. Excessive heat warning for Collin County. Temperatures above a hundred degrees. A heat index of one hundred and eleven. I don't know what a heat index is. It sounded serious.

"You've been warned," the warning said.

"I've been warned," I agreed.

Later I walked to Bob Woodruff Park. It was the day after the fourth of July. I wanted to see what Bob Woodruff Park looked like on the day after the fourth of July. Someone has said, about our time here on earth, that we might as well have a look around. I walked down Oak Grove, through the cemetery, past the horse stables where I've heard a certain young mare is owned by a certain real house wife from a certain reality TV show. There was a sign on the fence: "DIRT FOR SALE: $1 OR BEST OFFER." It was a hundred and three degrees out. Heat index of one hundred and thirty. I sweated through all of my clothes. Then I sweated through all of my clothes again. Then I threw up a little. It was, I had to admit, a little excessive.

"Well," I said. "I can't say they didn't warn me."

Whatever happens, you probably should have seen it coming.

As you'd expect, Bob Woodruff was covered in a bunch of Fourth of July crap from the night before. Firework shrapnel. Used picnic supplies. Detonated black cats and bottle rockets. The whole place smelled like gunpowder and Oscar Meyer footlongs. There was confetti and glitter everywhere. It looked like a warzone sponsored by Party City.

"Something happened here," I whispered to myself, low and serious, like I was in a movie. I'm always pretending like I'm in a movie. If I ever get shot in a mass shooting, I'll probably start acting like I'm Tom Hanks in *Saving Private Ryan*. That scene where he's bleeding out by the bridge. I'll do the whole thing, word for word, beat for beat.

"Earn this," I'll say to some stranger, grabbing them by the t-shirt, rolling my eyes all around in my head.

"Is this guy doing *Saving Private Ryan* right now?" they'll think. That's how spot on my performance will be.

I walked around the park until I got dizzy from the heat. Then I went home and shit my brains out. Excessive heat is a natural laxative. A generic-brand anti-depressant. I looked down after it was over and it was all old sponges and alphabet soup. Not the first time I've seen human brains splattered all over the place like that.

Ah yes, I thought. Just as I remember them.

They say if you've seen one human brain you've seen them all.

Standard vintage pasta salad.

100% interchangeable.

At night I sleep deeply and peacefully and have long, rambling conversations with J from inside my subconscious, outside the hippocampus, broadcasting live from No Man's Land.

"Do I seem happy at least?" I ask in the morning. "Do I, here at the midpoint of it all, seem content with the way things are going?"

Like most of us, I don't always know how I feel. And ¾ like most of us ¾ I don't always feel how I feel. That, as far as I can tell, is what psychology is for.

"And how are you feeling today?" a psychologist once asked me.

"Aren't you supposed to tell me?" I said. "What am I paying you for?"

In an attempt to know a little something about the way human beings work—in an attempt, that is, to not be a total moron when it comes to understanding the complex inner-workings of my thoughts and feelings—I've been reading Earnest Becker, cultural anthropologist from Springfield, Massachusetts. His National Best Seller *Escape from Evil* (1975). Follow up to his International Best Seller *The Denial of Death* (1973).

I'd read the *Denial of Death* a couple years ago, smack in the middle of the pandemic, when my denial was facing its biggest challenge yet. That book kind of fucked me up. Then I read it again. Double fucked.

A reverse evangelist: Earnest Becker came to tell us the bad news. The bad news is that we're all going to die. The other bad news is that we're all nuts. There is no good news.

After he wrote *Escape from Evil*, he told his editor to stick it in a drawer. Best for people not to know. You may recall: It was not sin that got Adam and Eve kicked out of paradise. It was knowledge.

"And do you know what he died of?" my genius writer friend John asks me about Earnest Becker, fucked up cultural anthropologist from Springfield Massachusetts, posthumous winner of the 1974 Pulitzer Prize. "Colon cancer. An agonizingly disordered shit mechanism."

In July a viral Twitter trend emerges: sexy Evangelical couples holding up hand-painted signs. "We will adopt your baby." A backlash to the backlash to the reversal of Roe v. Wade. The biggest cultural uproar in recent memory. Hashtag whatever.

Say what you will about Evangelicals but they're all smokin' hot. Fit and clear-eyed and tastefully dressed. They shop at Target. They drink smoothies. They're waking up early tomorrow and going for a jog. I don't know how we're supposed to compete with people who are so thoroughly and enthusiastically out of their minds.

"Faith is being sure of what we hope for and certain of what we do not see," the Bible says.

The DSM-5 has another name for this.

After work I go to the 1418 coffee shop in Downtown Plano. I've been coming here lately to work on a freelance project writing SPAM emails for a popular fitness app. A nice change of pace from my day job writing SPAM emails for an unpopular bank. It's easy-enough work. I make $75 an hour and don't try very hard.

Walking around money, I think of it as.

Per diem.

1418 is nice. Cozy and quiet with a soundtrack that's always featuring Ben Gibbard. I've heard the coffee here is good. I wouldn't know. All coffee tastes the same to me. Hot and brown and a little bit sour. I just shut up and drink it and accept other people's opinions about it. At 1418 it costs $4 plus tip. Comes in a stupid little cup.

"Yum!" I say when they hand it to me.

The other thing about 1418 is that it's always full of Evangelicals. I can tell they're Evangelicals because of how hot they are. They wear Polos and flip flops and ask about each other's weekends. Their weekends were good. They went to the lake. Despite everything I've known and read and experienced first-hand, I can't help but like these schmoes. They're friendly and soft spoken and good at listening. And they're so hot. I like how hot they are. It's weird to think that they're everything that's wrong with the world. I try not to hold it against them.

"Anyone sitting here?" they ask about the couch across from mine.

"You are!" I say and shoot sunbeams out of my face.

Recent news items: Man survives 18 hours at sea by clinging to a child-size football; The National Right to Life Committee's general counsel confirms legislation would force 10-yr-old rape victim to have baby; Biden approval ratings hit all-time low; New Fat Shack brings deep fried everything to Plano.

Recent text to J: FAT SHACKKKKKK!!!!!!!

Monday morning the geniuses over at NASA post a picture to Twitter of the deepest, darkest part of the known universe, captured in ultra-high-definition by the ten billion dollar James Webb Space Telescope.

"There it is," they say.

"There it is," we say.

Thursday afternoon my doctor emails me JPEGs of the deepest, darkest parts of my large intestine, all the way up my own ass, a place I have been slowly crawling for the better part of two decades, a little further every day, captured now in ultra-high definition by a miniature Go-Pro glued to a stick.

"Here it is," he says.

"There it is,' I say.

By mid-July it's too hot to go outside. According to J's Jeep's: four hundred and fifty-one degrees. The new No Man's Land. "This is no place for a standard vintage homo sapien," I think, stepping out onto my front lawn, looking around.

Saturday morning our energy company—a company whose name is French for "once more, with enthusiasm!"—sends an email asking all customers to set their thermostats little warmer than usual.

"Whatever temperature you feel comfortable at," they say. "Set it a little warmer than that."

Like most idiots, I usually assume somebody else knows what's going on here. I assume they have it under control. The most helpful thing I can do in any situation is follow instructions. We spend the day drinking Topo Chico and eating popsicles shaped like ballistic missiles. We close the blinds and turn off the dryer. Around noon I figure out a new trick. I lift up my shirt and lay face down on the hardwood floor.

"Hey come here real quick," I yell to J in the other room. "Come check this out."

At night we eat Fat Shack and watch *Mission Impossible V: Rogue Nation*. Like all of the *Mission Impossible* movies, this one's all about creative problem solving. It's also a little bit about holding your breath for six minutes straight in an underwater vault. I've seen it five times and it still stresses me out. Proof that you can know exactly what's going to happen and still manage to convince yourself that maybe you don't know exactly what's going to happen this time, that maybe you have no idea what's going to happen this time, that maybe this time ¾ all reason and historical evidence aside ¾ you're going to be surprised. It is, if you believe Earnest Becker, what all of us are doing every minute of our waking lives. Mowing our lawns. Making our grocery lists. Acting like we don't know how all of this ends.

"It's over when I say it's over," Tom Cruise says halfway through the movie.

"It's over when I say it's over," I whisper back to the screen.

At night the temperature drops into the low hundreds. The air conditioner runs full blast at 70 degrees. Thanks to our efforts and sacrifices the grid remains operational. Tomorrow we'll be asked to ration our water usage, but tonight the neighborhood sleeps soundly with a steady 120 volts of pure American electricity pumping directly into our fuse boxes. Not that I know anything about how electricity works. I know that it's zig-zag shaped and bright yellow. I know that it's sometimes used to kill people and sometimes used to bring them back to life. In Texas it costs twelve cents a kilowatt hour. The going price of power. Cheaper than dirt.

toby keith said it best

Max Dougherty

i should have been a cowboy.
i think i should have fallen in love
with the desert.

i'm a summer child and i yearn for warmth,
my horse and me moving as one, the
blue sky unfolding overhead.

i should have fallen in love with the knots in my
horse's mane. after a long ride in the wind,
i should know how to braid my horse's hair and
how to weave the strands to build something beautiful.

i should have learned to groom my horses.
i should know the muscles of my animal's body and
which joints needed support, should have learned
to appreciate and not just to admire.

it would have been nice to know the family business once.
i have had horses, a few,
i have loved them and i have learned them.
on a horse's back i know what to do; i was
taught to ride the horse before i knew
to walk.

i love the west, and
i love its wilds, and
i love the people who raised me, and

i should have fallen in love with the desert. i should
have done a lot of things, but
i fell in love with you.

John Prine Wears Midwestern Cowboy Boots

Matthew Medendorp

John Prine wore cowboy boots even though he was born in Maywood, Illinois which is next to Oak Park which is next to Highland Park which is next to Chicago. That's just three stops on Metra's Union Pacific West line from downtown, where Prine got his start playing in clubs after his day job as a mailman. Nobody in Chicago or Maywood wears cowboy boots really, but John Prine was Americana before Americana was a genre and his dad was from Kentucky, where I haven't spent much time, but I can say with a stereotyped certainty, is a state that people wear cowboy boots in. Maywood is six Metra stops from the Chicago suburb where I grew up, Wheaton, where I certainly saw nobody wearing cowboy boots, even people who rode horses didn't wear cowboy boots, they wore riding boots, the English type, cavalier and expensive burnished leather, the haughty kind of riding that showed horses for dressage and pinned up ribbons on barns more expensive than most of middle America's homes. Still, I've owned two pairs of cowboy boots in my life, maybe because of John Prine, so the leather of those cows or those pigs or whatever animal hide the bootmakers in Leon, Mexico use as a source material might hang on John Prine's conscious. Leather is a dirty business, but something has to be done with the hides of all that meat we eat. It's only economical. So maybe it's meat that's a dirty business, but the leather doesn't help. Better to think of them as inseparable. It could be that the boots I'm wearing were also a hamburger I ate, and it doesn't seem fair to blame John Prine for the hamburger I ate, even if I could blame him for the boots I'm wearing. The OB who attended my birth in Cleveland, Ohio wore cowboy boots in the hospital, as if he had traveled there on horseback in his white coat and stethoscope after a quick pick-me-up at the local swinging door saloon. So, there may have been undue influence on me from the beginning, a kind of predestined path for my feet to end up in a pair of calfskin Western wear. Though let's not discount that this Midwestern doctor with a flat Ohio dialect could have also been a John Prine fan, buying his first pair of boots after he heard "Angel from Montgomery" on the radio the very first time he cruised through the 1-80 traffic on the way back from a residency interview, flushed with potential success. And since then, this doctor has birthed generations wearing his trusty cowboy boots and used the proceeds of a long career in medicine to subsequently purchase more cowboy boots, each from a more far-flung source (python, caiman, ostrich) all while delivering generations of babies whose first near-sighted, placenta free visage in the world is not the loving embrace of their mothers, but the rich tones of exotic leather against a cool tile hospital floor, imprinting, like newborn ducklings, on the low heeled roper or the higher heeled classic cowboy as a parental figure. And once their auditory senses developed and into a pair of well-heeled boots of their own, once their feet grew and they established some semblance of fiscal independence, they eventually found their way to John Prine.

Space Junk Yard Junk
Margaret Grayson

Some kind of plant is growing out of the hood of my sister's white Mazda sedan. The car has sat beside my Dad's driveway, in between the fence and the firewood pile, for a few years, ever since Mary hit a deer—though she maintains that it hit her—mangled the front end and then bought a used SUV to replace it. The Mazda is driveable but ugly, held together with white duct tape. Dad parked it out of the way until he could get around to having the bumper and hood replaced, either to sell or to drive if his own car, which had just topped 200,000 miles, finally gave out. None of those things happened, and the Mazda sank into the clay, forgotten. Tires flattened, battery dead.

I imagine the determined weed working its way

up through the engine block in the dark, weaving through a maze of valves, winding around belts and wires, until it peeped into the sunlight. When we discovered it, we marveled at nature's tenacity. Nobody made any effort to move the car.

A decrepit car in the driveway or out behind the house is a pretty common sight in my dad's neck of the woods. The arid Colorado climate is well-suited to long-term automobile shortage because with a dearth of water and oxygen in the air, iron and steel don't rust. But rural yards across the country are decorated with beaters and buckets, lemons and shitboxes, clunkers and heaps. Scrap metal dealers paper local bulletin boards with handwritten fliers: "WE BUY JUNK CARS." People without trash service sometimes keep an old "trash truck" used exclusively for weekly trips to the dump. The trope has gotten the drawling Jeff Foxworthy treatment: "If you mow your lawn and find a car, you might be a redneck!"

Of course, not every yard car is an abandoned backup. In the U.S., at least, it's common for someone, usually male, to have a vehicle into which he pours his spare time and mechanical skill. Whether the car runs, whether it's a classic Mustang or a vintage Ford pickup or a tuned-up Honda Civic, is irrelevant. What matters is the keeping of it, the fussing over it, the doting on it. There aren't many things that the tradition of American masculinity allows men to be truly, embarrassingly lovesick over. Cars, like lawns and sports teams, are one of them. For those who don't have a garage, the project car gets a prime spot in the driveway; see the popped hood, see the man with grease on his hands, see all that could be yours with a little hard work.

In that context, it makes sense that in December 2017, Elon Musk, the 21st century's premier shitposter, announced he would be launching his car into space. Maybe when a person reaches the status of billionaire, he can only justify his excess of capital by removing himself from the scale of humanity. The universe becomes his backyard and the only reasonable stage for his posturing.

The car in question was a 2010 Tesla Roadster, slick and shiny and red like a pomegranate seed or a woman's manicured fingernail. SpaceX engineers mounted it like a hood ornament, convertible top down, to the top of the company's Falcon Heavy rocket. In the driver's seat sat a mannequin dressed in a space suit; in the glovebox there was a copy of the *Hitchhiker's Guide to the Galaxy*; on the circuit board there was inscribed a message to the aliens who read English: "Made on Earth by humans."

In February 2018, the rocket and car launched and established a solar orbit just outside that of Mars. A four-hour livestream video of the car and spaceman dummy looked, like most videos of space, as though it had been filmed in front of a green screen, the spaceman's eerie stillness highlighted as the car floated past the sterile, cloud-marbled earth. Today, the top YouTube comment is distinctly yearning: "It looks so peaceful. No politics, no media, no drama, just peace and quiet."

Business websites fawned over Musk's marketing genius. Who needs a billboard or a magazine spread or a Superbowl commercial slot when the universe is at one's disposal? When the Roadster in the sky can signal wealth and humor and capitalist excess not just to the blinking masses down below but to the entire cosmos? The world's billionaires have entered a full-blown space race while down below, systems sputter.

Not that Musk's car, currently traveling at 74,000 miles per hour some 183 million miles from here, has an easy road ahead. If meteorites don't destroy it, some scientists predicted that the sun's unfiltered radiation would eat away everything but the car's metal frame and glass windshield within a year. The spaceman will probably disintegrate, but the skeleton of the vehicle could last for thousands of years out there. We won't know its fate for a long time, because the Roadster's orbit won't come close to ours until 2047. But its lack of visibility almost doesn't matter. For most of us, outer space exists primarily in our imaginations, and much to my personal dismay, we cannot forget the car out there among the twinkly lights any more than we can forget the man who put it there.

Back on earth, I've always associated my father's house and property with the sheer volume of stuff contained there. Furniture and mementos in the basement. Mismatched linens and the vestiges of my sister's and my teenage wardrobes in every closet. Tools of every variety in the shop. Leftover hay and bags of sheep's wool from our farming days in the barn. Dad's not a car guy but a boat guy, so he owns a tin-can fishing boat (maximum speed: six miles per hour), a blue plastic kayak from Walmart and a small sailboat that we dream of taking to the lake every summer but never quite do.

Such collections cannot be contained by architecture. The stuff spills out into the yard: Two desks with broken shelves, a fallen clothesline, and, inexplicably, an authentic Chicago fire hydrant, heavy as sin and buried among the tall grass. Some of the detritus is obviously useful, representing future plans and dreams. Some of it we might burn in a big pile come winter, always a joyous occasion. Some of it "needs to go," as my dad would say, but never quite left. All of it is chock-full of spiders. Once I took a photo of a broken iMac computer in a trash pile, struck by the way that sleek white-and-silver frame, such a monumental purchase when new, was tossed in alongside an orange pool noodle, the leg from a dining room table and a leaky watering can. Junk is junk.

Getting rid of things is hard and, in many cases, expensive, involving the borrowing of a truck and the 30-minute drive to the dump. In some cases, as with cars, scrap metal dealers will come and retrieve the dead vehicle, but there's still a certain level of effort involved: calls to make, pickups to be arranged, emotional ties to be severed. Dad works full time and spending his days off dealing with the clutter is not usually a priority. It bugs him, but not in an existential way. He would love a universe where the yard is free of flotsam, where the Venn diagram of stuff he owns and stuff he needs forms a perfect circle. But this is not the universe we live in.

Dad's former neighbors, wealthy Texas transplants, fretted (audibly) that he would bring down their property values, but there wasn't much they could do about it. Not so for our other old neighbors a few years back, renters who accumulated an incredible amount of junk in just a few short months at a house nearby, the yard becoming a maze of scrap metal. Then one day they abruptly started cleaning up, hauling stuff away. Word got out that they'd been ticketed for operating an illegal junkyard. The Texans had called the county.

There's no one to call to report an excess of space junk. The solar system lacks zoning regulations. Since the 1950s, people have been blasting objects through the confines of our atmosphere into the great vastness beyond, and not all of them come back. Many spacecrafts are intended to stay out there indefinitely, housing astronauts, taking measurements and photos, wandering the pitted surface of the red planet next door. But for every functioning spacecraft, there are thousands of dead satellites and bits of debris deliberately shed or torn off those craft in the rollicking ride through Earth's atmosphere. The U.S. Department of Defense is currently tracking more than 23,000 pieces of space debris larger than a softball in Earth's orbit. Objects in low orbit move at around 17,500 mph; at those speeds, even flecks of paint can cause damage to other spacecraft and threaten astronauts.

Defunct satellites and space stations also continue to orbit and slowly degrade. Countries including the U.S., China and Russia have used anti-satellite weaponry to blow up their own satellites, creating more debris, and then publicly condemned one another for doing so.

My aversion to space junk as a concept and my derision for Elon Musk's contribution to it boils down to the fact that I feel bad that the sky, like the earth, is becoming downright crowded with human inventions. The proliferation of satellites in our skies—SpaceX alone plans to launch thousands for satellite-based internet services—will be visible at night, forever altering our view of the stars.

But said internet services will bring connection to populations around the globe that other broadband companies have disregarded. And when it comes to the junk: Who am I to talk? Every piece of plastic I've ever bought or used—every toothbrush, every tampon applicator, every scrap of bubble wrap—is still here. Just because it's in a dump somewhere doesn't mean it went away. And, as my dad's yard demonstrates, there's plenty of it that we don't even bother to get out of sight. Space junk operates under the same principle as yard junk: it's there because getting rid of it is too expensive or too hard. Wherever human beings go, we can't help but litter.

I sometimes joke that minimalism is for rich people, just like launching cars into space. Packaged as both an aesthetic and a lifestyle, minimalism promises purity, clarity and peace through lack of clutter. Tiny houses filled with beautifully designed multipurpose items, timeless capsule wardrobes, airy downtown lofts with no signs of mess or life: all these highly postable images seem the domain of those privileged enough to throw things away knowing that they can always just buy them again. (Not to mention that my attempts at minimalism always serve to make my life more boring. Every few years I purge my closet of random items I rarely use and then find I have nothing to wear on Halloween.)

The broker people get, the more they seem to hold onto things. It's impossible to know when that box of newspapers or mismatched tupperware might come in handy. The older I get, the more I appreciate working class resourcefulness, the kind that always has twine or scrap wood or spare tires on hand, the kind where you never have to worry about whether you have the right size Phillips-head screwdriver— only whether you can find it.

Still, I have my prejudices, and a yard car isn't a great look. I worried that the parked Mazda indicated that my dad had crossed a threshold into a new level of redneckery that would be difficult to return from. Dad didn't share my concerns, having long ago given up on caring what people think of him.

Then, last June, my grandparents offered me their old Subaru, which was about five years and 50,000 miles newer than my current car. I gratefully took them up on it, but fretted about what to do with my own loyal and beloved hunk of metal. My old car wasn't worth more than a grand and would be hard to sell because of a loud rattle from the back end that I'd chosen to ignore for months. But we weren't sure the Subaru was entirely mechanically sound either, so the idea of keeping the old car as a backup was comforting. Dad offered the obvious solution. "Leave your old car here," he said. "I've got the room."

So I did. I parked it next to my sister's Mazda,

and went away for grad school. I promised myself it wouldn't be forever, that no plant life would have time to take over. Next summer, when I'm home, I'll figure out what to do with it. That's what I keep telling myself.

Going to California

August Edwards

I

Danny Says

Music & words by hotel tap water

It's my seventeenth birthday and mom bought me a bouquet of flowers from Kroger's, a tender image in a bitter January. Days prior, my family locked the doors to our home in Connecticut forever, after months spent purging two-thirds of its contents. Foreclosure imminent. One sacrifice in moving to California. My first time moving there. Before my birthday, I asked if we could stay longer with my grandmother rather than continuing the 3,000-mile drive.

Little Green Apples

Music & words by Stone Lake

LaPorte, Indiana is less than one third of the way from Connecticut to California.

Act Naturally

Music & words by ice

Take Illinois. Not Chicago, either. The unending cornfield graveyard—a frozen ocean. In January everything begs to keep its life. Like Robert Plant simply says, "Goin' to California with an achin' in my heart." The aching sparks visions of a gold coast—ghostly electrostatic mystery.

Starlight

Music & words by flat Pepsi

Wind sways the van. There's a dusty Taco Bell in Bumfuck Nebraska, ninety miles from a Holiday Inn one way, seventy miles from Exxon Mobile the other way. Bales of hay, bales of hay, and bales of hay. How can I know life exists if I'm only looking from the highway? I am squirmy flesh on the interstate.

The Ride

Music & words by peroxide

There's an Outback Steakhouse in Wyoming. The "seasonal vegetables" consist of the following: carrots. There is a young woman with bleached hair in the booth across from me at the cowboy state's steakhouse, she is sitting with two older men. She is talking about how she wants to move somewhere

where she can pursue her dream of becoming a model. She says there's nothing in Wyoming.

All My Favorite Songs
Music & words by grease
McDonald's wrappers and hamburger bun crumbs—dinner drops to the van floor. We spend money we might not have had on hotels and motels and Arby's roast beef sandwiches.

Cranked up Really High
Music & words by spring water
Distressing fog in Utah. It smells like dead fish in Salt Lake City. We get a hotel room and we order Pizza Hut and the pizza guy's hair is lime green and his tattoo arms reveal little of his peach skin. The closer we get to our enigmatic destination, I fight with my little brothers about bedrooms. It's when I spill hot gas station tea in my lap that a certain resentment towards California mounts in me, and it feels like losing, and I can't stop fighting.

Flowers on the Wall
Music & words by A&W root beer
We eat notably bad KFC in our new home before we retire to our air mattresses.

II

I'm Not a Loser
Music & words by an empty cup

I don't want to take off my necklace, the one my grandmother made with a piece of her mother's rosary. Showering is the worst part—I've been skipping showers—because that's when I have to take it off. I wonder if there will be a day when I can say "Once upon a time, I couldn't take off that necklace." I had to move to California again.

Purple Rain
Music & words by dehydration
My necklace has a magnetic clasp, which worries me, because what if it gets tugged off when I sleep? It's got wire wrapping with purple pearls— my grandmother's take on rosary beads, though there's not 59 of them, and there's no crucifix either—and in the middle is the piece from the original rosary, a relief of Mary, and purple quartz where the cross should be. It's a frankensteined sort of family memorial that pacifies like a blanket.

I'm in Love with My Car
Music & words by leaking orifices
When I got dumped, I had to pack up my things from his house so I could begin the 16-hour drive to my new- but-not-so-new home—a 16-hour drive where I would think, for 16 hours, *will I ever make this drive again?*

We'd been doing long distance and I was in the middle of visiting him, which turned out to be the end of visiting him. Until that point, I didn't see my presence in California as truth. My purple beaded rosary necklace was the first thing I grabbed in what was a sort of grasping-at-a- token-of-love moment. It'd been on a shelf above the head of his bed in a limp heap. Why I ever put it there to begin with, I don't know.

Christian Woman
Music & words by the desert
In the high desert, I worked at a Christian bookstore—we carried all genres, though, and I loved the owners. I'm not Christian and neither is my grandmother. On a day where nothing else really happened, my boss noticed the necklace and said she used to wear a rosary as jewelry before she realized it was cultural appropriation. This sticks with me but I don't know what to think about it.

I've Just Seen a Face
Music & words by ripples
My patinaed Mary makes a promise to me until I realize I must make a promise to her. Detached from her original beads and dethroned from her perch above the cross, I feel like I'm allowed create this new meaning. I cling to her like she is the great-grandmother I never met but know.

Foggy Mountain Breakdown
Music & words by wine
My grandmother once saw me wearing the necklace she made years after she gave it to me. She said, "Now where did I get that piece? Must have been the antique store," about the relief of Mary. I said,

"You told me it was from your mom's rosary." She said, "Right, okay—I guess I need my glasses." She motioned for me to take off the necklace so she could inspect it. "Bring that back to me one day and I'll fix it up for you." I didn't know there was anything to fix.

Be Yourself
Music & words by a joke
My necklace is mine. My hair tangles in the wires that are wrapped around each other. My hair becomes wire. My hair is so broken, right there at the nape of my neck.

Going to California
Music & words by sinking
Kingman, Arizona is about halfway between the Central Valley and Albuquerque.

Hello Darlin'
Music & words by a stranger
Kingman, Arizona and I have a funny relationship. There are sister Best Westerns right across from each other on Andy Devine Ave. and I've stayed in both. Once alone and once not. The last time I drove through Kingman I was alone again, and I couldn't stand the thought of being in one of those Best Westerns again, so I stayed in a Ramada that was Route 66-themed. Even though, when I first got there, there was a man complaining that there was hair in his "fresh" bed, I liked that Ramada the best of all. The view of the desert, beyond dirt mounds and miscellaneous trucks, was like a soft watercolor

painting. The walls of the motel were crowded with murals of the stars—Elvis, Charlie Chaplin, Godzilla, and Andy Devine himself.

Do I Ever Cross Your Mind?
Music & words by liquor rings on a coffee table
I think about the Wendy's around the corner from my grandmother. I can see it from the balcony of her apartment.

Clocks and Spoons
Music & words by just a drop
I heard my grandmother stole *her* grandmother's ring from a casket. She took it from her mother's finger, there resting in that casket. The ring—simple in design, gold with a small nugget in the center—had already begun to smooth with wear. My grandmother was 19. Years later, she passed the ring on to my dad, and my dad gave it to me. Neither of them seems close to death. "Look," I showed my grandmother once it was on my pinky. "Oh, well there it is! Now—how did I ever get my hands on that? How did I get that?" and since we were sitting at a loud dinner table at the time, I had to yell back so she could hear—"Dad said you snatched it from your mom's casket."

Faith
Music & words by my body
In Kingman that very last time, that was the first night I slept with the necklace on. When I settled

myself in the car to hit the road the next morning, as I said goodbye to Kingman, I clutched my throat when I had an inkling it might be bare; but the necklace was there, and I felt so good in that moment. So good I swear I saw the cartoon portraits on the Ramada wave goodbye to me, so good that now I can't take off the necklace.

Here's Looking at You
Music & words by a reflection
It was 5pm, dark, early January, when he was done with me for good—said he wasn't invested in the relationship anymore. The week before, he accidentally broke the sideview mirror on my Honda Civic. It dangled useless like a dislocated shoulder. He tried to mend it with duct tape. He would've paid to fix it if I asked. He would've let me stay 'til morning if I asked. He never told me no, but maybe I never let him.

Fake Plastic Trees
Music & words by a dry well
It took him two full days to dump me. That was definitely all my fault, too. For goodbye, I kissed him on the cheek, and he said, "Thank you." That's what he always said when I
kissed him on the cheek. I guess it became a reflex.

III

Stories
Music & words by drought

Follow this little thread, please. My grandmother's apartment has been her apartment for over 30 years. The building's called Bellevue. It's in LaPorte, Indiana.

Her mother, whose ring I have on my pinky now, had a tumultuous relationship with the man who impregnated her at least four times.

Over 60 years ago, she planned to flee to California with her second son. My grandmother, the youngest, the baby, who was living with her lovely, lonely aunt, heard about the plan and begged to come along.

She remembers her wool skirt, how it was too hot for southern California.

It was only for a year.

She speaks about that year vividly, but it takes years for her to admit that she felt like an unwanted addition. This left her wrought with guilt for decades, a sliver of her reality trapped in her childhood. And she felt unwelcomed when she returned to Indiana, but it was always her home. And she is my home. That's what I feel when I put on her necklace, too.

I Never Get Lonely

Music & words by plastic

Empty coffee cups, crunched water bottles, straw wrappers and a wrinkled Mento's sleeve. Star Wars sunshade I bought because I thought it was stupid. This is what's in my car, plus me, and now this Impossible Whopper from Burger King in New Mexico. I'm sorry, don't know which town, just know I'm westbound.

Pay No Mind
Music & words by the Rio Grande
Goodbye is physical until you let go. Goodbye is a show. The real goodbye never comes, it only leaves with quiet disintegration. Transition from presence to memory.

God Only Knows
Music & words by gin
Every year I've lived on this earth I've had to endure at least one goodbye with my grandmother—I've had to leave her, leave her apartment, only to return to wherever temporary return. How many songs are there about saying goodbye? I think most songs are about saying goodbye, one way or another, to some entity or another. I'm reminded of someone who said every story is definitively a love story. Every goodbye with my grandmother is ripe with the promise of saying hello again.
Against Ergonomics
It shouldn't comfortably fit the hand. It shouldn't feel as though it has become a part of your body. It shouldn't be comfortable to hold. It shouldn't guarantee hours of use free from fatigue.
It should not disappear. Nothing should not seem to stand between the user and the goal. The thing should interpose.
It is alien. It is wrong-shaped. It has its own reasons for being the way it is. It never lets you forget. It resists.
It is better at its intended purpose than you are at yours.

Nine Essays

J. Robert Lennon

Against Ergonomics

It shouldn't comfortably fit the hand. It shouldn't feel as though it has become a part of your body. It shouldn't be comfortable to hold. It shouldn't guarantee hours of use free from fatigue.

It should not disappear. Nothing should not seem to stand between the user and the goal. The thing should interpose.

It is alien. It is wrong-shaped. It has its own reasons for being the way it is. It never lets you forget. It resists.

It is better at its intended purpose than you are at yours.

Cow

We agree that, at some point, we should bring the baby to see a cow. But when? Not now, when all new experiences are equally puzzling, and the baby has no understanding of what should and should not amaze her. And not later, when the idea of farm animals has grown familiar, and a cow will come as no great surprise. We should bring the baby to the cow at the very moment a cow will blow her mind.

I told my students this should be the goal of their stories. To lure the reader into a state in which a cow will blow their mind.

Custody

I hadn't heard from my student in a while. I seemed to remember I was one of his thesis advisors, but if I had been, surely he would have sent me pages to review. My memory must have failed me.

Then my colleague called. The student had told her he'd been emailing me drafts for months, and that I'd been ignoring him. This wasn't so—I hadn't gotten these emails, nor the attached writing.

As it happened, he'd been sending the emails to someone else with the same name as me, a custodian in the school of agriculture. I wasn't the one who had ignored the emails, he was. Perhaps email wasn't even a part of the custodian's work for the university—it could have been that he was assigned the address automatically, and had never even opened the inbox.

Or perhaps the custodian had received my student's novel. Maybe he read it, but decided to keep his opinions to himself. Or maybe he'd sent my student comments, but to the wrong address—the address of another member of the university community, one with the same name as my student. Maybe this person used the custodian's comments to revise the attached novel manuscript in his own way, entirely different from the way my student would have revised it, had he been given my advice, or even the custodian's advice.

When my student finally sent his manuscript to my correct address, mine, I briefly entertained the notion that it was this version I was reading—the one altered by the name-sharers' chain of custody—rather than the one I would have received had my student addressed the original email correctly.

I felt bad for wishing it was.

Kreskin

The Amazing Kreskin was a family friend—an acquaintance of my grandfather's, and an occasional dinner guest at my grandparents' on Sundays. In the seventies, when I was growing up, he was a frequent guest on The Tonight Show, and a skillful and charming magician and self-described "mentalist" whose signature talent was an ability to compel people to behave in unusual ways.

One of those people was my mother. In the last days of her pregnancy with me, she allowed Kreskin to hypnotize her. Afterward, he said she would experience no pain during the birth.

It worked. My birth was swift and painless. Afterward, recuperating at home, my mother felt a compulsion to call Kreskin. She didn't. Minutes later, the phone rang. It was him. He said, "Why didn't you call me?"

*

Fifty years later, my wife turned to me and said, "Do you think Kreskin is still controlling your mother's mind?"

Neighborhood (III)

I went out to the porch to water the hanging plants, two Boston ferns. The plan was to take each down, set it in the yard, and spray it with the hose. As I came down the steps with the first plant, a woman approached, walking a dog down the sidewalk. I said, "Good morning." She ignored me. Went back up the steps for the second fern and when I turned around, the dog was pissing on my fern. The woman just stood there, right in front of me, watching her dog piss on the fern. Then she and the dog walked away.

Raymond

My grandparents had a shirt made for me, printed with a number—I don't remember which—and the words JOHN ROBERT, the name they liked to call me by. It was my favorite shirt. I was eight or nine.

One consequence of wearing the shirt was that the neighborhood bully had begun calling me Raymond. The version of my name printed on the shirt had marked me as beloved, thus open to ridicule. It was necessary to twist and taint the name, to hurt me. There is nothing wrong with the name Raymond, but it isn't mine.

I was riding my bike around the neighborhood one day, and passed the bully, and he shouted "There goes Raymond on his gaycycle."

Many decades later, I think of this phrase, spoken in the bully's needling voice, far more often than I think of my grandfather's voice calling me John Robert. When I ride a bicycle now, I think, "There goes Raymond on his gaycycle." I also think of this phrase while driving a car, or just walking. I speak it aloud, quietly. It feels more true of me than of almost anything else that's been said of me, for its preternatural ability to have gotten under my skin. I can picture the gaycycle: not my actual childhood bike, but a glorious assemblage of glitter and rainbows, and pink streamers trailing from the handlebars in the wind, and a pride flag hoisted on a fiberglass post.

I imagine myself accepting a major literary prize. The trophy, for some reason, is a crystal decanter full of port. And a brass nameplate bears not my name but RAYMOND ON HIS GAYCYCLE.

Sheet

I dream that the fitted sheet has come loose and I can feel the bare mattress with my toes. I wake up to discover that it isn't so—the sheet is secure.

I'm disappointed with my sleeping mind for generating such trivialities. Then, later, I'm impressed; the dream wasn't trivial at all. This kind of disorder—a messy blanket wedged between sofa cushions, a tablecloth five degrees off true—bothers me all out of proportion to its importance. It stands in for types of disorder that I'm powerless to control.

My sleeping mind knows me well. It doesn't need to serve me fascism, sickness, storm and fire. A loose sheet will do the trick.

Thread

My wife and I decided to have a child, or children. I already have two children, adults now, from my first marriage, and I thought I was done with the chaos of early parenthood, but it seems that I've decided to invite it back into my life. Or, rather, I've decided to inaugurate a second iteration of the life of parenthood. It feels akin to traveling into the past. Yet it makes me feel old—about as old as I actually am. I wonder if my body will remember the tasks of those years—holding a child on my shoulders, changing a diaper—or if they'll again seem risky and new.

This time around, conceiving a child will require medical intervention. I find myself at the doctor's office, where the doctor, an energetic, talkative man in his forties, is repeatedly driving a needle into my testicles. He did this once before, a year ago. The latter portion of the process failed, which is why I'm back. The procedure he's performing requires a light touch, he tells me. I've been locally anesthetized, but not quite enough.

To pass the time between sorties into my

reproductive organs, and to distract me from my discomfort, the doctor and I resume our conversation of a year ago, about the renovation of the rental house he owns. Last time, he was laying down wooden floorboards. This time, he is installing a microwave oven.

"It's the kind that goes under the cabinets," he explains, glancing at the door that a nurse will soon come through, to inform him he has to plunge the needle in again. "I drilled holes in the bottom of the cabinet so I could feed the bolts through." He wiggles his fingers. "I could feel 'em in there, poking out, but the holes on the microwave were in a little depression. The bolts didn't go far enough to catch the thread."

He gazes at me, shaking his head. I think he's smiling, but I can't tell, because of his mask. It's pandemic times, and we're all wearing masks.

"So I had to shave off some of the wood," he says, making a gesture nearly identical to the one he made moments ago with the needle. I imagine the tool he must have been holding then—a chisel or plane, I assume. His hands have traveled back in time, repeating the work. "Then the bolts caught the thread and I was good to go."

The nurse comes in shaking her head, and bearing a tray with another needle on it. The doctor takes it up and says, as he said just a couple of minutes ago, "Okay. This one's the keeper."

Test

The psychology lab at the university invited me to bring the baby in for testing. When I arrived, a graduate student took the baby away, and a different graduate student led me to another room. There, I was asked to sit at a computer and play a video game.

In the game, I was stranded by the side of a busy highway running through a forest. I'd been tasked with caring for three friends' infants, and all three were strapped inside my broken-down car. One by one, I was to bring each child out and set it down on a blanket from which it would attempt to walk or crawl into traffic. My job was to flag down passing cars while protecting the children from those same cars, which never stopped, however energetically I flagged them.

The computer was old, and slow to respond to the commands I clawed into its keyboard with increasing desperation. My heart rate increased as the graduate student sat off to one side, taking notes. The room was windowless and dirty and my eyes stung from the dust and sweat. When the game was over, I was not told whether I had done well. I was thanked for my participation and assured that the video game babies had survived the ordeal.

When I emerged, rank and disheveled, into the light of the main office, I found my daughter laughing and rolling around on the floor among a pile of toys. She was given a gift for her efforts, a charming tee shirt. Her graduate student caretaker informed me that she was a delight and invited her to return anytime.

She had passed the test.

In the Dust

Sage Marshall

Dust. Dust chalking up the sidewalk. Dust in the dense July air, making our mouths grimy and dry. Dust and rust. Rust eating away at the tubular tin statues of exotic animals positioned at the three main intersections of the one paved road that ran through the center of Norwood: A tin elephant, a tin hippo, and a tin moose. Running down the sidewalk on the way to the San Miguel County Fair, my little brother Luke and I paused briefly to clang our fists on the hollow statues. What were these tin creatures with broken hinges and frayed metallic limbs doing in a cow town on the western slope of Colorado?

At the Norwood Fairgrounds, the prize-animals were kept as dust-free as possible. The cattle—corralled in small pens, their necks tied with thick rope to the fencing—were doused in glitter. The pigs were fat and round and full. They, too, sparkled as they snorted and rammed their snouts through the dirt floors of their small pens. The unsheared sheep were plush and white as a shag rug. The goats, with small horns jutting out their heads and hair like silk, bleated, reared, twirled, and kicked their stubby staunches. The bunnies wore blue and pink bows around their necks. Standing next to them proudly were the girls who'd bred them. The chickens—even the chickens—were primped and primed. Their speckled plumage was vibrant with color. I held my mom's hand as we milled around the fairgrounds. Enthralled but slightly taken aback, I was too scared to touch any of the animals. I didn't know if I was even allowed to and didn't want to look like a clueless outsider by asking. And I didn't want to get my fingers bitten.

The other boys wore worn cowboy boots smeared with mud and dung. Hours of work out on the prairie had burnt their once-pale skin scarlet. I wore sunscreen and brand-new Old Navy cowboy boots.

We lived in Telluride, a ski-town 40 miles away, which was nothing like Norwood. We had snow. They had dust. I'd only ever been to this part of the county when my dad, brother, and I went fishing for crawdads at Miramonte Reservoir, a lake 20 miles down Specie Creek Road.

My dad was enamored with Louis L'Amour's writing, which, like the spectacle of the rodeo, presents a romantic view of the West. Driving down two-lane highways to my sports games in nearby towns, he and I listened to L'Amour's books on tape, read to us by gruff-voiced actors. The stories, though the names and face changed, were all the same at the core.

Start with a cowboy. He might be an inexperienced

ranch hand or a mysterious old gunslinger. Either way, he's got the stuff: the grit, the gumption, and the stubborn streak of independence. One of the most telling representations of L'Amour's cowboy-hero—in all his many incarnations—comes from the short story "War Party." Bud is an untested boy of about thirteen in a wagon train heading west. When others in the expedition decide to turn back "with their tails betwixt their legs" in fear of Indians, Bud and his mother keep their resolve. In a showdown with one of the older men in camp, Bud defends his mother's honor, proving his manhood. L'Amour connects this courageous behavior to the land itself, writing that "when a body crossed the Mississippi and left the settlements behind, something happened to him. The world seemed to bust wide open, and suddenly the horizons spread out and a man wasn't cramped anymore."

I wished this was true. I moved to Telluride from New York City when I was seven. It took a while to fit in. Almost all of my classmates had been there since they were born—raised together in this small town. I ran across the ridge of snow and went skiing with everyone else. I played hockey, soccer, basketball, and baseball. But I had trouble finding acceptance from my new classmates.

When dusk arrived, we migrated with the crowd over to the oval arena adjacent to the fair. The sun dropped beneath the horizon, and the stadium lights buzzed on. The fairgrounds of a town with a population of 572, not counting the livestock, transformed into a full, expansive world—one I didn't understand. Men lassoed and tackled frantic calves. Women spun their horses around barrels in a manic tango. The bulls and the broncs bucked, raising clouds of dust. Dust that glowed in the yellow light. The cowboys barely managed to hang on for more than a few seconds. The spectators cheered and stamped their feet, while eating burgers, hotdogs and shelled peanuts, drinking soda pop and beer. Watching with everyone else, it didn't seem to matter that I'd never lassoed a cow or pressed a red-hot iron to the rump of a squirming calf. When the show ended, we walked back to our Chevy Blazer behind a group of tall men with cowboy hats perched atop their narrow bodies. They dug their hands deep in the pockets of well-worn jeans. The soft clatter of spurs was the last music I heard before I dozed off on the ride home.

I didn't know any better.

My dad always liked to mention how L'Amour had a ranch just a two-hour drive away from Telluride. L'Amour's stories were of the landscape we wanted to claim as ours. My dad didn't wear a cowboy hat or do anything so dramatic, but he'd always say "howdy" when we encountered anyone wearing a flannel shirt in places like Norwood. They'd often just say "hello" in response. It embarrassed me when my dad did this. He'd never said anything like this when we lived in New York. In contrast, L'Amour's cowboys were confident—sure of their places in the West.

Not only is L'Amour's cowboy sure he belongs in the West, he's also fearless in the face of marauding

Indians and cutthroat ranchers. He doesn't complain or make excuses for himself. He puts up with pain, whether it's caused by a gunshot wound or a dust storm. He doesn't talk about his—or anyone else's—emotions. Instead, he proves himself through action. And he always—always—comes out on top. I kept him in the back of my mind on the soccer pitch, when our coach shouted at us not to hit the ball with our purses. And on baseball field, when our coach taught us not to be afraid if a careening, hard-hit ball came our way, but to grab it with our bare hands or block it with our chests. After listening to L'Amour on the car ride before a game, I stepped onto the field with grit and determination. Like a gunfighter poised for the draw.

Yet, L'Amour's stories soon started to bore me. I was comforted by the familiar endings but also frustrated. I'd read enough books to realize that there were other possibilities for stories beyond L'Amour's formulaic plotlines. And I sensed there was something off about L'Amour's cowboys, even if I couldn't fully express what that something was. I was intrigued by Native Americans in a romanticized way, and I found myself cheering them on in L'Amour's stories.

While everything always turns roses for the cowboy-hero, the same can't be said for the indigenous people or women in L'Amour's writing. I could tell L'Amour was telling simple, one-sided tales. In his Sackett Series, which my dad and I often listened to, he valorizes the conquest of the West, book after book, one patriarch at a time. The entire series is about one white family settling the American frontier. I had an inkling there was more to the story.

Meanwhile, I wanted to go on adventures of my own.

We arrived at the rectangular ranch house on Wilson Mesa next to a rolling pasture with four horses. Sunlight kissed the trio of Wilson Peak, Wilson Mountain, and El Diente in the distance, but it had yet to reach the mesa. I jammed my hands in the pocket of my sweatshirt as Brian's mom, Susan, tried to call the resident of the house. I didn't understand why she didn't just knock.

Brian turned to computers at a young age where, I think, he could find solutions that he couldn't socially, which is to say that Brian was even more peripheral than I was. He didn't play sports with us. He didn't become a part of the group. Still, Brian and I would often spend summer days careering through sloping single-track on our hard-tail mountain bikes.

Brian and I wandered into the pasture towards the horses. Brian's mom was friends with the What had looked like pristine rolling grass turned out to have a layer of mud beneath it. We found ourselves trudging through the muck in our sneakers. We didn't have cowboy boots and were wearing shorts. We hollered at the horses, then tried waving our arms like we were directing an airplane on the tarmac. Nothing. Every time we seemed to be getting close enough to the horses, they inched further away from us. And it wasn't like we had anything to rope them with or to lead them back to the pasture's gate if we did reach them. We were ankle-deep in muck. The land around us was big and wide and open—waiting to be ridden through—and we couldn't even reach the horses 20 yards away.

Back at the ranch house, Susan had started wandering around the outside of the house. Brian and I began to trudge back. Then we heard a door bang open, and a man's voice erupted. Who's there! He was shirtless and peering out the screen door of what must've been a bedroom. When he realized who it was, he softened. Why didn't you just knock?

In a few short minutes, he donned a red and brown flannel shirt, a pair of jeans, and his Stetson. He brought a rusted tin can filled with some pellets of horse feed out into the field. Two loud shakes of the can in the crisp morning air and the horses were nibbling from his palm. He cinched the saddles down so tight that I worried they might suffocate the horses.

Soon I was perched atop a spotted gelding and felt the breeze whipping my hair. I used one hand to guide the reins and pressed my heels against the horse's rump to make it run. The man stayed back at the ranch house, while Brian, Susan, and I plodded in the direction of the mountains, which were still far off in the horizon. By the time we trotted into the next pasture, the Colorado sun had spread its warmth across the high-country plateau. I led the way, pushing my horse at a slightly faster pace than the others.

The cows were spread out in a long, shallow ravine when I saw them. I whooped, my voice cracked, and I jammed my heels harder into the horse's sides. The horse entered a rocking lope down the slope—directly towards the herd. Spooked by us, the nearest cows began to flow down the ravine in a river of cattle. It was a dream. I was playing cowboy. How simple.

Then I reached a bulky, muscular bull that stood there looking at me, snorting and scraping one of his sturdy hoofs against the ground. I pulled on the reins and slowed to a halt, wondering if the bull would charge at me or turn tail if I pressed on.

In farms and ranches, male animals are raised for slaughter, which is to say they are fattened and killed as soon as possible. Farmers are pragmatic folk. They save themselves the trouble, the trouble that is a male animal. A rooster will peck a hen to death. This is part of the pecking order. A boar will gore another boar if he is allowed his tusks. And bulls lock horns and butt to establish dominance. Female animals— the moms—are the ones worth preserving.

What makes a bull become so aggressive in today's world? Scientists offer three reasons:

1) It's a natural part of their social order.

2) They've been bred for aggression for generations, for strength.

3) Bulls are often isolated from the herd.

In Norwood at the County Fair, bulls had rubber bands strapped around their balls before they are ridden. This made them buck and gyrate, with the male riders mounted atop them.

And have you heard of a *sidewinder*? Sometimes instead of killing bulls, ranchers slice their dicks at an angle. When a sidewinder mounts a heifer, it's unable to "hit its mark." The proper term for a sidewinder is a *non-entry teaser bull.* They are useful for identifying cows in heat, which the ranchers can then impregnate by hand. Ranchers should use young, vigorous bulls for this, because it's important they be—or at least had the potential to be—sexually active.

Before we went to the ranch, the middle school librarian recommended a Western that quickly became one of my favorite books. Larry McMurtry's *Lonesome Dove* is a sprawling story that begins in dust. Sharing the title of the novel, *Lonesome Dove*, a small town on the Texas-Mexico border, is "for most hours of the day—and most of the months of the year…a town trapped in dust, far out in the chaparral flats, a heaven for snakes and horned toads, roadrunners and stinging lizards, but a hell for pigs and Tennesseans." From here, ex-Texas rangers Captain Call and Gus McCrae embark on a cross-country cattle drive.

Lonesome Dove is a critique of, and an ode to, the classic L'Amour-style Western. Captain Call is the stoic, even-headed cowboy-hero you'd expect. But he's no hero. He's the unwitting and unwilling father of a young cowpoke named Newt Dobbs, who he had conceived with a local whore named Maggie. Even though everyone else in the cattle company knows and wants Call to own up to his paternity, he refuses to. Instead, he gives Newt a horse named "Hell Bitch." The horse goes on to kill Newt. Unlike in L'Amour's West, the wide-open land of McMurtry's novel doesn't free his cowboys, it brings out their flaws.

The other useful thing about a *teaser bull* is that

they can gain weight in the summer they're used for identifying fertile cows and then be easily killed off before winter. Profits maximized.

McMurtry's novel is still rife with Western clichés. Call and McCrae are more-or-less your typical cowboys. They aren't put up on a pedestal like L'Amour's cowboys, but they, too, can't escape the masculine norms of the American West. The ever-prideful Call refuses to acknowledge his paternity of Newt. McCrae injures his legs in an Indian attack. The doctor amputates one leg, and McCrae wakes up to find that the other is also infected. But he doesn't let the doctor amputate it. He'd sooner be dead man than a gimp.

Bullshit.

Speaking of, the bull stared right through me. I didn't dare press my horse further down the ravine. Then I heard Brian's mom calling me back, desperation in the harsh edge of her voice. What did I think I was doing? I turned the reins in retreat.

The bull stayed where it was and started grazing again as we walked our horses back to the ranch house. Susan drove us home. My legs were raw and red from rubbing against the saddle. Brian and I hadn't even thought to wear jeans.

After that escapade on the ranch, I stopped reading Westerns for a while. I'd grown tired of the repetitive nature of most of them. I no longer felt like a misfit in Colorado. But when I went to college on the East Coast, my interest in The West was renewed. Again, I felt different from my peers, most of whom were from New York City or Los Angeles and didn't spend much time in the outdoors. Instead of trying to fit in, I leaned into my Colorado persona, which I hadn't realized I'd developed. I couldn't stop talking about the deep-blue sky and vast expanses of wide-open space that still remained out west.

I soon convinced my friend Wesley, who's from Miami, to go on a weeklong road trip through Wyoming. We spent a few days in June backpacking through the high-country of the Wind River Range, scrambling through remaining snow bluffs and dodging grizzlies, clinging tight to our bear spray all the while. Then we drove on to the Tetons and spent a couple of days sleeping under the star-dappled sky in my mom's old Buick Rendezvous.

On a fall day back in Connecticut, Wesley and I sloshed through the rain to see *Brokeback Mountain*, a movie based on the short story by Annie Proulx. Larry McMurtry wrote the screenplay adaption. Jack Twist and Ennis Del Mar are spending a summer watching over a herd of sheep in a remote area of Wyoming. Twist is a wanna-be rodeo star whose father introduced him to rodeoing, but who never supported Twist when he tried his hand at it himself. Del Mar is a gruff, quiet cowboy who's engaged to a girl back home. Alone on the range, they develop feelings for each other but are hesitant to explore them. Eventually, though, they fall into a fervent affair. Then the summer ends, and they part ways.

Both men go on to marry women but are still drawn to each other for brief "fishing trips," when they'd spend a few days reunited in the wilderness.

Twist, though, wants more. He wants to share a ranch with Del Mar. But Del Mar refuses to fully acknowledge his feelings, let alone act on them. Even when his marriage dissolves, he won't be with Twist. He's haunted by the grisly murder of two gay men who lived on a ranch near him when he was a child. So he spends his days as a cowpoke, driving everybody away. Meanwhile, Twist is killed for being a faggot. The movie ends with Del Mar, alone, in a trailer out on the wind-swept range.

Walking out of the movie, Wesley said he appreciated the character of Del Mar because he knew so many people like him, out of touch with their own feelings. Watching Del Mar made me tense. Why was he so self-centered in his stubbornness? Why didn't he change when he realized the damage his behavior was inflicting on Twist, his wife, and his daughters?

Still, I saw parts of myself in Del Mar. Closed off. Tending towards distance. Pushing down memories and emotions instead of working through them. Ignoring how my pent-up anger and sadness can impact others. But even though I empathized with Del Mar, I couldn't stand the way he kept making the same mistakes. Again. And again. And again. I wanted to punch him in the face, to jar him into realizing his mistakes. But I knew that wouldn't solve anything, only being more of the same. Smashing fists. Breaking bodies.

How can we get beyond this version of a "Western man?" Even in a story that explores man-to-man intimacy under Wyoming's star-dappled sky, the confining masculine norms of the West triumph in the end. How can we imagine possibilities beyond this?

When I think back to that road trip with Wesley. There was potential for tender physical affection between us, but we ignored it. We slapped hands and wrestling playfully like brothers. Proximity through play-acted violence. He prodded at me and waited for me to react and push him around—and I did. Then at night, we smoked weed.

Stoned and dozing off in the front seats of my mom's car, Wesley's whole body suddenly jerked forward, startling me, too.

"Are you ok?" I blurted.

"Yea, I just felt like the whole sky was falling down on me," he said, gulping for breath. "It was a dream, or a hallucination, or something."

Consider this an anti-myth.

The summer following that one, I returned to the San Miguel County Fair with Wesley and my girlfriend at the time, Maile. The animals were doused in glitter as usual. This time, I didn't have any qualms about touching them, even though Maile and Wesley were more hesitant. But it wasn't anything special, grazing the rump of a glittered cow, touching the horn of a glittered goat.

After the fair wound down, there were a couple of hours to go before the rodeo began. I'd planned on taking Wesley and Maile to the Lone Cone Saloon for burgers, but the place was shuttered for good. Dust on the doorknob. Dust on the sidewalk. Dust in the air. Even the tin animals were gone. The only real life on the main street seemed to be at the two liquor stores, which were within a block of each other. We bought two PBR tall-boys and a hard cider then headed back toward the car. On the walk back, we passed the local grocery market. Outside, a man was smoking baby back ribs at a big, black smoker. He offered us each a sample rib; one bite into the juicy meat, and we decided to buy a whole rack. The man put the fresh ribs into a plastic container like any you'd find at a superstore. We bought a carton of strawberries for dessert. Sipping our drinks along the way, we hit the road for a sunset picnic at Miramonte Reservoir.

We parked and walked over to a small picnic table, where we plopped down and guzzled the ribs as hordes of mosquitos buzzed at our calves and forearms. Despite the bugs, we were at peace. Small waves rippled across the surface of the lake. A bald eagle circled above, hunting for trout. It didn't even cross my mind that the ribs we were eating came from pigs just like the ones we'd just been admiring.

Before we left, I walked alone down the shoreline. I accidentally stepped on the sun-bleached skeleton of a dead crawdad, and it splintered into white shards beneath my hiking boot. I peered into the murky water, searching for the dark green back of a live crawdad, like those I'd caught years ago with my dad and little brother, but I didn't see any.

We returned to the fairgrounds and paid $10 bucks a piece to enter the rodeo. The locals, wearing cowboy boots and big metal belt buckles, milled around eating hamburgers and Frito Pies, drinking

16-oz tall-boy Bud Light cans. Most of the guys wore NRA, American Farm Bureau, or MAGA baseball caps. Their pale faces blushed red from the booze and excitement.

I'd worn a t-shirt, a pair of loose-fitting Levi's, leather hiking boots, and a sweat-stained baseball cap—not quite a cowboy, but not too far off. We bought beers and found a spot to sit in the metal bleachers.

The sunset turned the loose dirt of the arena a deep gold as the riders swished through it atop their horses, kicking even more dust up into the burning sky. We oohed, we aahed, and we stomped our feet with the rest of the crowd. Everybody laughed when two sturdy corn-fed high school football players spun in ten circles and dizzily sprinted in a short foot race. Only one bronc rider had made it to Norwood for the small rodeo. He was a veteran who had served two tours in Iraq, said the announcer. A country boy who'd defended his country. A true hero. And even though I didn't believe in the war, for the moment, I believed in the hero.

The chestnut bronc bolted out of the gate, arching its whole body electric under the stadium lights. Our hero perched on the horse's back, holding the rope attached to the horse's neck with one hand and waving the other behind his head in performed nonchalance. He leaned back and jabbed his star-shaped spurs against the bronc's bulging front shoulders, drawing small streams of blood. He didn't wear a helmet, just a well-worn cowboy hat, with the brim tilted down so low his eyes were in shadow. And somehow, despite the horse's irregular bucks and spins, throbs, and gyrations, he remained atop the bronc, a partner in a violent pas de deux. Then the horse made one unexpected turn, jarring our hero off balance. Then another. And another.

But he didn't get thrown off completely. His leg was caught in the saddle. He dangled from the side of the horse. I could see the terror in the whites of the bronc's eyes, and I heard its rapid snorting, sending tendrils of dust into the air. Dust I could taste. Dust in my throat. The bronc bolted along the edge of the arena, blasting the man against the metal railing over and over again. I put my hands over my eyes and hunched down in the stands as though it was a bunker. But I couldn't look away. Peeking through my fingers, I watched the man's body go limp as it ricocheted between the horse and the railing. The rodeo clown tried to slow the bronc but couldn't. Two bodies careening. Thrashing, body to body to metal. Men from the stands hopped the fence and rushed into the ring, charging in a ragged cluster towards the rampage. On foot, they looked like children compared to the big bronc. Eventually, though, the mass of cowboys cornered the horse and ripped the limp body from the saddle. An ambulance drove over to the body. Away from the action, the bronc loped out of the stadium.

"I swear to God I'm going to kill that bitch," yelled one of the men who'd helped corral the bronc. His face was red, and a pistol jutted from the holster on his hip. He struggled towards where the horse had disappeared. Two other men reined him back by the shoulders.

"It wasn't the horse's fault. You know she didn't do it on purpose," said another man. The tumult died down quickly, and an uneasy quiet pervaded the arena. People murmured prayers and tried to peer past the paramedics for signs of life.

"Do you think he's dead?" I asked.

"No idea," said Wesley. Maile was silent. The minutes stretched on as night settled in. A cool breeze tugged at my bare arms. I gazed up to the sky but couldn't see the stars, only the mean yellow of the dust wafting under the stadium lights.

The clapping came slowly at first. Hesitant. I glanced back and saw a man covered in dust. Dust and blood. He shooed away the paramedics trying to help him and limped slowly across the arena, stirring up yet more small clouds of dust with each halting step. The clapping escalated into a low roar. I took a deep breath but couldn't bring myself to join the cheer.

That night, when we walked back to my car before driving home to Telluride, I didn't listen for the music of clattering spurs. I didn't gawk at any silhouetted cowboys. I thought about the jagged-edged spurs pressed against the bronc's smooth, sweat-slicked hide, drawing bright red rivulets of blood. I heard a body pounding against a steel fence. Again. And again. And again.

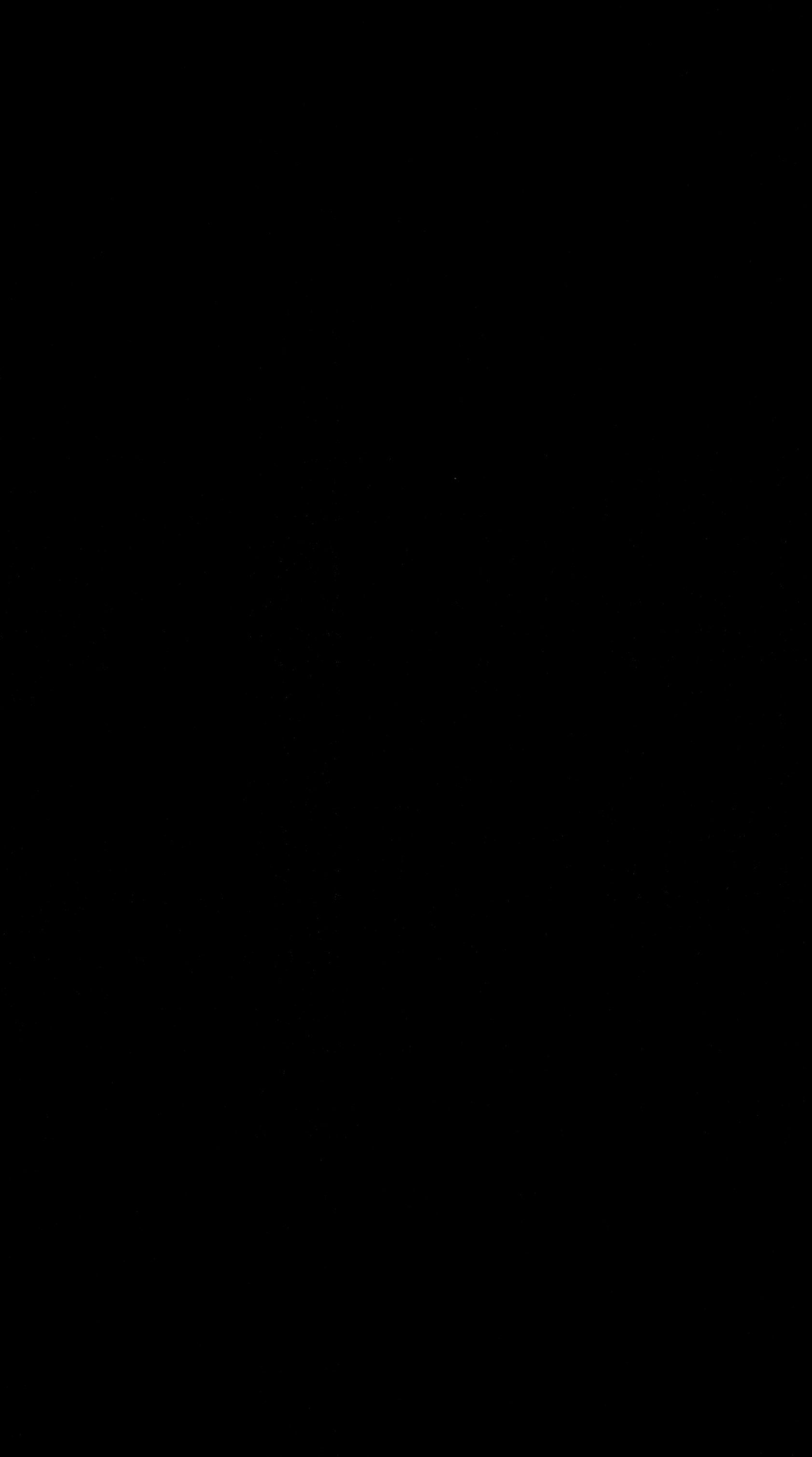

Silicon Valley of Heart's Delight: All This Used to Be Orchards

Sarah Lyn Rogers

Once, inside a house I did not know, I opened a door and everything was dirt. It was a normal interior door, leading to the only room accessible downstairs. But the room wasn't a room. It was the underbelly of the floor above, a giant pile of soil backlit by slits in the wood foundation. The home-viewing in Oakland, California had already felt strange. Other than a staircase leading to the dirt room, the first floor was walled off, creating two separate units—one with natural light and a real kitchen, and the other, a mold-trap carpeted unit with considerably less in the way of amenities.

Three friends and I were looking for somewhere to live. One had just had his rent hiked up to something he couldn't afford alone; I was tired of strangers being able to touch the window five inches from my sleeping head, so close to my apartment's car port. We wanted space to breathe, a washing machine of our own.

But the dirt room filled me with an ancient dread—something about outdoor light haloing the soil-pile through unfinished wood slats, and the damp earth smell behind a normal hallway door, outside inside. The dirt room was the upstairs' crawlspace—a nightmare word—but tall enough to walk in. *What kind of house has this for its secret center?* I remember thinking. *You could hide something terrible in here.*

*

Set in Milpitas, California, John Darnielle's new novel, *Devil House*, is, on one level, about a man named Gage, a true-crime writer and alleged descendant of royalty, who moves into an infamous house where some terrible murders occurred decades prior. But what struck me about *Devil House* is how it seems to implicate the real estate market, sinister and culpable, in the crimes that occur. In this book, people are murdered, but the closest we come to a villain is "a local slumlord named Evelyn Gates." Inheriting property from her father after his death means she considered herself rich, just as she'd always considered her father rich: collecting rent every month in places whose tenants didn't have enough leverage to demand repairs, tenants who lacked the social standing to assert their right to a plumbing upgrade or to functional wiring in every room.

Evelyn Gates has her targets, her marks: the perennially at-risk, people with bad credit who knew when they signed the lease that cleaning deposits were a scam but who lacked the standing to object.

California wants you to intone it and conjure a montage: Hollywood sign, crashing waves, smog-rich sunset, redwoods. The campus I attended there was dotted with palm trees, in an area known for drought, an area that has a *fire season*. This is how California advertises California, what it wants to be in the collective unconscious: manifested abundance, tropical oasis in the desert.

But the California I remember is dry-grass hills along the highway, burnt golden, a look like the smell of dust; along El Camino, streetlight poles with mission bells missable amidst fast-food drive-thrus and auto shops, the orange signs and cones of road construction, rags tangled in spiky weeds near an on-ramp. Chain-link fences. Driveway dirt. Highway curiosities: the Flintstone House, van on a pole, the hulking giant Babe the Muffler Man. The California I remember is always being on the way to somewhere else. In brochures, California looks like arrival. In my life, it has looked like moving toward but never reaching.

In its depiction of the unsung everyday details, *Devil House* portaled me back to the Bay Area, where I grew up. Darnielle imbues Gage with the lived experience of the place, one that knows how, if you talk to someone over fifty who's lived there all their life, they'll remark that "all this used to be orchards." That's the whole statement. I've heard it all my life, spoken as though its implications are obvious, though they aren't to me. Sometimes it sounds like regret for an unrecoverable past, or admiration for the speed of change, from the Valley of Heart's Delight to the Silicon Valley. Maybe it's the gravity of witness. Someone handing me their memory: once, our whole economy was fruit.

*

Finding a house with friends was an attempt to start a new part of my life, one in which I was no longer a student and could figure out who I was. I hadn't yet realized that "who I was" was an equation, what was left after habitual subtractions. For class, I'd turned in story after story about claustrophobia, loneliness, dead ends, my *what you know*. I didn't know why I knew it. It was a song that played inside. Or a song that played outside and woke me up, me, the guitar on the wall that vibrates when it hears one of its strings' own notes.

House-hunting was often absurd. Something advertised as a bedroom would have a closet and then enough floor space for a twin bed touching every wall, nothing more. Realtors would lie, say it's a single-family dwelling, then you'd get there and discover they meant only the top floor for the four of you. As though you'd see the place and fall so much in love with half a house that you'd forget.

*

In *Devil House* (and in its novel-within-the-novel, *The White Witch of Morro Bay*), Gage researches the perpetrators, sketching out their reasons for squatting in an abandoned building, or falling in with bad influences while avoiding the home they had. For some, the home they had was where they were trapped with an abusive father or other poised-to-explode relationship. The home they had was the place where they did battle, could not recover strength. The ad-hoc home they *choose* is fortifying but precarious. In a building and neighborhood where everything used to be something else, Gage tells us this is really a story about "restoring ancient temples to their proper estates."

*

Ten years ago, the South Bay went through a phase when city developers apparently wanted to revive white stucco, orange-yellow, red tile—Spanish Mission style, new old. This was before the newer city developers, who've made apartments and townhouses out of gray and lime-green Duplo blocks. The California I remember is a smattering, a dragging forward, aspirations toward style but never a cohesion, default-font signage on old businesses jammed up against the neon logo of a franchise, land of prospectors and speculators.

*

Investment property boggles my mind. In the free market, based on voluntary exchange, if people don't want a particular seller's good, they buy from a different seller or opt out. People can't opt out of needing homes.

*

The eponymous Devil House that Gage moves into wasn't always a house. He tells us it had been a sandwich shop, a diner, a newsstand, and a porn shop before becoming a hideout and de-facto home for people with nowhere else to go.

There were a few cursed locations in my hometown. But the mundane sort of cursed. At the corner of Homestead and Las Palmas, a white brick building with a tile roof and a parking lot lawn has lived a few lives over the past fifteen years—as a burger place, Mexican restaurant, a seafood grill, currently a Taiwanese restaurant. At the corner of El Camino and Los Padres, a drive-thru teriyaki place became two different Indian restaurants and is now abandoned. Even the coffee house where I first heard Darnielle's music, at the corner of Stevens Creek and Lawrence Expressway, once an open-mic haven, has changed owners and name, changed owners and name again, is nothing now.

*

At my palm-tree dotted campus, men in my classes wrote stories in which men triumph in tired ways, with bizarre psychological implications classmates would barely address. These fictional men defended their cuckolded honor by being *really good* at chess; accompanied their fathers for the first time to a strip club and received their first lap dance, a gift paid for by Daddy; and were amazing hunters but beat their cave-wives with clubs because, look, toxic masculinity used to be a real problem. My stories were quiet; the characters I wrote wanted so little. At the end of class, the strip-club author approached me and said, "The takeaway from your story was just *I matter*." He said it with a sneer. Like it would be humiliating for someone to hope to know that.

*

During one of the stretches of my life when I was rarely alone in my home, I liked to drive to Linda Mar beach in Pacifica, place of rocky cliffsides, the Pacific Ocean, and "the most beautiful Taco Bell in the world." I'd go there just to look from a cliff of sand and pickleweed at the too-cold water, let the sight and sound etch-a-sketch-shake me back to some essential essence.

*

We finally found a place, the four of us, near the San Francisco airport, somewhere with both a yard and a washing machine, which felt like winning the lottery. When I excitedly told my family that our application was approved and the place was ours, they asked me how much it cost. They were outraged, then softened, voices full of pity for naïve little me. I've never *heard* of a house so expensive, they said, as if they had any idea. As though I had made the worst possible choice, and not the only viable one. As though I personally had been scammed, and not that the whole thing is a scam.

In the back yard, which was half gravel pit, half lawn, tea roses climbed the fence. I can still remember their pink scent. For a while I felt like someone new in the light and physical space months of effort and the random hand of fate had bought me. Then crept in tense energies and unspoken, unspeakable rules. Sometimes a house is just a house. Often it's a tiny governing body and economy where the person furthest from precarity has outsized say.

*

I think there's a dirt room of sorts at the center of many—maybe most—households. Something everyone who lives in it can feel, that tugs at their awareness with disquiet. It's there even if you never open the door.

*

On a rental application, you don't matter. You are not a you. You're an unknown variable in someone else's investment, a liability until the investor deems you a worthy risk. You're your social security number, bank account number and statement, credit score, employment letter, paystub, and maybe the answers to borderline illegal questions about debt and family planning. What matters about you is your earning power, which is the same story you've been hearing all your life, only so naked there. To a large extent, your earning power is determined by forces outside yourself, what someone else deems you deserve. Here, too. You submit. You submit yourself for approval and maybe you get it. Maybe next time.

*

In Millbrae, near the BART station, fennel sprouts up wild, all along the asphalt path bordering the bay—a home hemmed in by wave-breaker stones and carefully laid sod. A living thing makes whatever work.

*

I'm fascinated by how much of *Devil House*, a crime thriller, confronts property, people, and the stories we tell ourselves about both, stories we believe about what people deserve. In *Devil House*, there are lots of devil houses, not just the sites of murders.

*

If you picture a multi-million dollar home, do you picture a celebrity mansion, bungalow in the Hollywood hills? Something overlooking the ocean? Would you believe me if I said that it's the market rate for a single-story three-bedroom house on a sleepy suburban street in my hometown? I barely believe me. All this used to be orchards.

January 9, 1973

Maya Lowy

Pieces of

(what had been)

Cindy

still faceless

muscled tibia

thumb with painted nail

begin

to wash up

along

the shores
of the Monterey Bay

In This Poem, Strawberries Symbolize Sensuality & Abundance

Allyn Bernkopf

I am imagining us in Ogden, Utah.
We are sitting at Talisman sipping

strawberry champagne. The couple
next to us keep leaning over, asking

how on earth we ordered those drinks
in a beer bar. The woman is on my side,

the man on yours. She nestles her forehead
in the dip of my clavicle. He keeps

squeezing your shoulder & claps your
back. Your eyes thistle every time

he does it, & she and I are laughing.
The reason they join us is because

of me. I showed her an app—"I Am"
affirmations. Told her if she says them

enough, belief sprouts like vines across
the skin, the heart, the lungs, the gut.

I read her some of my favorites: *I am
worthy. I am strong. I am waiting for*

*true love. I am worthy. I am strong. I
am enough. I am enough. I am enough.*

The woman wants to believe me but argues
it's too abstract. She needs something

to grip, something to swallow, something
to breathe in—I imagine our flutes are empty

after all this, so I take the strawberry out
from the bottom of my glass, carve it

into four slices & distribute a piece
to each mouth, a communion. *I am*

strawberries, I say. They argue the seeds
are too small, too few, but that's not

the point. I get to you last—place
the fruit in the bowl of your tongue,

tell you to chew. When we sit, our flutes
refill. You & I are beside each other. A new

strawberry rides the bubbles at the base
of the glass & you are holding my hand.

In This Poem, Backpacking Symbolizes Constancy, Eternity, & Stillness

Allyn Bernkopf

Big words, I know, but listen to this: we
just parked at the base of Naturalist Basin

    Trail. This is the second time we've done
    this & it's my favorite. The trail is just

        under 15 miles roundtrip, so you lace
        your ankle boots tight & I snug up

my chacos. You hold each of our packs
in each hand—weighing who's heavier.

    We unpack & repack to distribute the weight.
    You take out the canned wine & I put it right

        back. You argue it's unnecessary heaviness
        but I know we'll enjoy it up top. You're happy

about this later. The trail takes us through thick
pines & a valley of ash. *There was a wildfire*

up here a few years ago, you say. *Burned*
for miles and miles and miles. It was started

    by humans or lightning. There are so many,
    now, we can only blame a single fuse. Walking

a landscape of ash is strange, though. We talk
about how it feels like treading angel food

    cake. About halfway up, we stop for snacks—
    Nuts, fruit, dark, salty chocolate. People can't see

    us because we've gone off trail. Or, if they do,
    they think we're something dangerous. Cougars

do stalk these parts. When it's recognized we're
human, they laugh. We laugh. It's fun to pretend

    real fear—The next few miles is technical. The dirt
    is slick, rocks are loose, trail is narrow. On top of all

    this, the sun is starting to sit lazily on the horizon.
    No one wants to be stuck on a trail like this

in the dark. Luckily, we get through & it opens
into a mountain meadow. There's an alpine

    lake & a river so clear, we can see the fish
    crowd beneath boulders. Tomorrow, we'll return

    to catch & release. Our campground is still a mile
    or two away, so we keep going until we see Blue

Lake. It's dark now, but our headlamps illuminate
small circles in front of our bodies. We are at 11,000

    feet of elevation now so I can't hold my breath
    for longer than four seconds. The only reason

        I notice this is because it's July 2020. We find
        a spot to camp. Someone else formed a fire

pit, so we hunt for wood nearby. Fire formed,
we set up our tents and prepare for dinner.

    You are the most prepared backpacker
    I know, which is why dinner is already pre-made:

        pre-cut veggies and hobo-dinners wrapped
        in foil. We toss them on red coals & within

twenty minutes, our bellies are warm. One
of the best flavors of campfire food is nearly

    everything has spice of wandering ash. After,
    we spend a good amount of time trying to toss

        a rope over a high branch to hang our food. You
        know. Because of the bears. This becomes

a game because I am 5'4" and you are 5'2"
and that branch is at least 15 feet in the air.

    Eventually, after much laughter, we get it.
    Sitting back by the fire, I bring out the wine.

You agree the wine was a good idea. I agree
the trip was a good idea. We talk & giggle deep

into the night, sisters together. In the morning,
we pack up & return to the river. Catch & release.

The Honky Tonks at the End of the World

Tina S. Zhu

The weather forecast says the world is ending via asteroid strikes tonight at ten Central Time. You and your ex Miranda Ming, the one you fucked in the dark last night for the first time since the breakup, pile into your dust-darkened Honda, setting course for Dallas. Dallas is a twelve-hour drive away, and you'll get there in time because Miranda woke you up at five by throwing a pillow at your face.

She puts on a country playlist to wake you up. You hate country music. It's all the same, you'd always say, as if your favorite pop power ballads about first love weren't. Honky tonks and pickup trucks and cold beers, Miranda sings in that nasal imitation Southern accent. Or maybe it's real—your cousin Brian's from Arkansas and has the accent, maybe Miranda picked it up too because there were no other Chinese girls in rural South Carolina. She takes over at the rest area filled with bleary families traveling to see their grandparents and cousins one last time, playing hooky from work and school because today's the last day, the final chance for one last hurrah. You crack open a beer gifted to you by a family having a makeshift picnic by the broken vending machines, excited to see two non-resting bitch face women with whom they could pretend to be friends. Miranda makes fun of you for being just like the heroes in her songs, broody anytime before noon. She's wrong—no Chinese girl would drive a honky tonk when a Honda Civic would do.

Today's just like old times, she says, tying her hair up again. Your car still smells like pizza. And where'd all the dust come from?

It does not smell like pizza, you say. You chug down the beer even though it's too warm, because you don't need her making fun of you for being a wimp. And what dust?

Whatever you say.

The car is silent until you pause in Memphis for lunch. Miranda insists on barbeque. You're not the biggest fan, but you offer to pay. Who cares about a little extra credit card debt if there's no tomorrow? When you broke up the first time, Miranda accused you of being too stingy, with money, with time, with emotions. You dollar-and-centsed every tiny gesture of kindness and every gift. In the four years since, you want to say, you broke up with another girl after she called your Happy Meal display shelf childish. But you keep silent, pour more sauce on your pork ribs.

Miranda just asks, Do you want me to change the playlist?

I don't mind, you say.

By the eighth honky tonk song, you take the wheel again. By the twenty-third cornfield, Miranda is asleep. By Dallas, traffic slows as the sun sets, the sunset to end all sunsets hazy with fumes from infinitesimal cars shining like stars from outer space. By nine, you make it to the drive-in theater and buy your tickets for viewing *Bill and Ted's Excellent Adventure* and the impending apocalypse. Dinner is a McDonalds' drive-thru. Miranda insists, saying this is the perfect chance to commemorate all the times you went together to complete your Happy Meal toy collection. You stick your nose in the bag to drink in the sweet, sweet scent of Chicken McNuggets and fries. You lick your fingers after finishing off the fries, desperate to get those sodium crumbs in your system after your last supper. Miranda watches, the end of the world forgotten.

You're not so bad, she says. Not anymore.

Great, you reply, stuffing more fries into your mouth and checking your phone for the time. It's 9:57 PM, you declare. We're almost there.

In the final three minutes, you lose yourself in the movie, laughing when Miranda does, watching from the side as she puts up her hair the same way she would when you'd marathon horror movies so you could cling to her during the scary scenes. When the movie stops and the shooting stars streak across the sky, brighter and brighter, you see the reflection in Miranda's eyes. You reach for her hand. She doesn't push you away. You close your eyes, because she was always the brave one.

The Fly

Devon Bohm

Today I am small and rusty and caged
in my own mourning—or is it actually
resentment, or loathing, or something more
winged and unbelieving like that feeling
you get right before someone lets all
the rules fall away? Open your mouth
for the desert's feast: roadrunner and
swallowtail butterflies, wasps fermenting
in the figs but no alcohol to numb you
in this clear, cold night of dirty dreams
and tar-caked promises we won't
remember making, won't be able to keep.
Mourning who? Mourning what?
It is, of course, in our natures to die,
dissolve, collide as starlight in the eyes
of those we tried our absolute best to love.
This is the driftwood, the flotsam, the debris
left over from a life well lived and loved:
to be outlawed from the mind of your
beloved, lest she lose whatever gifts
the desert's cool, shuffling hands see

fit to deal her. You weren't supposed
to die, but you were always a rebel,
weren't you? Is this dumb luck or
the spider's web? To be so bruiseable,
to have always been so ready to have
everything inside me sucked out to be
empty, empty, the shell of something
that once had its own pair of wings?

Hunger

Devon Bohm

Sweetgrass, dandelion, milkweed:
protection, health, and poison
I saw in the park today and I am
here to tell you about my own
understory. Picture me eating wild
mint from our yard in California
when they were cremating my father,
standing in the once-a-year rain
and devouring. Does death open
everyone's throat, or just mine?
You can overdose on anything,
even your own desire, even
when you retrace your steps
to find they lead to someone's
empty crypt. He died but he never
decayed, and I ate and ate all
the mint leaves, the honeysuckle,
the weeds we called sourgrass,
and the crab apples almost too new
and tart and hard to bite. The world
was feeding me, tenderly, tenderly,

and I was, I am still the greedy child
who only knows to want, who will
drink each storm down to the last,
echoing drop, who is still mourning,
still grieving, still eating her way
through all I'm given and can grab.
Sweetgrass, dandelion, and that
milkweed, reedy and deadly, torn
into pale, white clouds by my needy,
grasping, ash-dirtied, small, small
hands.

Lost Lake

Devon Bohm

Every spring,
a lake in Oregon drains
completely
into a 7-foot-wide hole
and becomes a meadow.
Every winter, it fills again.

Everything is cyclical, even this:
me grieving you,
your loss my own collapsed lava tube,
honeycombed and hollow
where everything goes to drown—

beetles and overripe blueberries
with their strange, dark juices like tarry blood
and everyone else I couldn't revive.

One day, I will follow the footpath
to the gaping maw of the earth.
I will watch my grief disappear
and everything will bloom.

One day, I will believe
I don't miss you
for a moment.

But nature knows:
what drains must fill the heart again.

It's the price of living on this earth.

You Have a Bit Part in a Cowboy Film

Rebecca Ferrier

He walks square, a muscular dog
with kneecaps made for doorways, wide
as entrances make a man wide.

His presence a full glass, foaming.

He is the protagonist in a cowboy film,
the old Westerns with a saloon door
that swings for as long as it takes
a man to die.

He is a man

who goes out at night to meet women.
I would like to be a man
who goes out at night to meet women.
Be the sheriff or the whoremonger

or the man with a pistol
or the man with a pistol
or the man who loses his pistol
at high noon and takes another pistol from
the man with a pistol
who shot him.

He walks square into a bar and he's walking to me,
his presence an empty spittoon filled
with spit, foam and petticoats, lifted.

He is the protagonist in a cowboy film
and I:

can ride a horse backwards,
point and shoot with the best of 'em,
have seen every film set in a whorehouse,

and I linger in shot for
as long
as he passes.

A Horse Who Also Jumps

Evan Nicholls

A horse who also jumps
jumps in addition to running
and carrying a person or
sometimes two,
carrying bags of water,
carrying food and things
for preparing a fire and camp.
A horse who also jumps
is great and so is a horse
who only carries and walks
and drinks from the river
after and before you
ask it to cross.

Horse Wearing Gas Mask

Evan Nicholls

I'll be frank: I am playing gin rummy with a horse. We are next to the road. The horse discards a day. The playing cards are letters from home. Word is 'They Are Dead.' Now the ghosts stop to watch the game. The gas mask is wearing a horse. The mask discards a day. The ghosts say, 'You Have Fifty-Two Pen Pals.' They say, 'We're Being Frank.' I let out a whinny. Isn't all that scary, we say.

Language Without Vowels

Dee Engan

Immigrants often move here expecting a better quality of life, and for Line that's materialized in fatter paychecks leavening the temptation to consume as elites did back home—everything, but moderately so, yet everything "moderate" by a difference: an excess greater than what she can express to her family abroad. So locals should feel grateful they can beef over dinner tables, for have these civil war patriots seen children in bikinis serving "beef" at the corner fresh?

Though when another freedom dies, Line touches grass as to not compare a depression between broken arms and stubbed toes—except her nation aches from foreign affairs, and its neck sinks deeper into corruption by locals who misunderstand how good their breaks go, snapping right whenever the law steps in while her people, in poverty, get stepped on, begging for a news report's attention.

If ever tempted to complain, Line speaks gibberish that wears high heels and upper-middle trappings of aspirants from the diaspora's breath, "the struggle," "the paperwork," "the educational system," "melting pot," "I love it," her own heels shattering on "work ethics" as another glass barrier appears.

The car?

It's new, from the Third World, tropical money—wickedness, locals claim, an ancient dowry she's showing off to proclaim her corruption. As Line drives to the polling site, houses grow in passing capital appreciation, minimalism by maximizing expenditure, with the smallest houses costing ten times her tenement.

She could go back home.

Nevertheless locals here need prodding on how to vote. Like Holstein cattle, they're too much gridlock gunmetal, playing off an orange more red than saffron rust—resentment's buildup fueling the afternoon's protest, blue worry regarding a loss of grazing rights.

Apparently, males eat twice a female's weight, plus floods stifle the corn and barley, leaving kochia to poison the calves, while healthcare's glow radiates greed's sheen; taxes, lower them, as each person's due is controversial altogether, how much, when, by whom, and until military herds the country safer.

That true? Really?

Even a polemicist will use language without vowels: marshmallows on clickbait, enough chewiness to sweeten the melt about graveyards serving nationhood under distinction. Or else BIERGARTEN, BIERGARTEN, BIERGARTEN offers combo meals at affordable prices. Try the lager with some schnitzel, tenders, spoil of resentment to spike any stomach: saliva drinks, hair through pasta elbows from a migrant who distills problems by backwashing complaint on cheese, but not in your backyard, don't worry, they're far enough that only the brim of a hat dare greet you.

So when plastic wrap runs their table out of space to the corners, Line starts, onion, cheese, the lid falling off from a container, bicuspid on bell pepper, molar down whenever her canine chases after bread crumbs. Then Ruby says, "Tell me you hate this country. I know people who've served. Tell me you work too much or you have tons of coworkers and bosses you wish you could shoot in the back of the head."

Though she, like many here, had her wisdom teeth pulled early.

Wildfire fumes drag open the doors, placing Line to drive a leg of another hunt. She fiddles the GPS slung on suburbs, that sushi joint selling roe next on intersections where cattle roll coal and protest rises against smoke, election day's treat, fervor against the tear gas hecatomb, carcasses, which Line resurrects, using a their own trick: white pickets around farmhouse meadow, real life moderation over seamless meme brain butchery crank on the lever of their truth, beef's authentic, lived experience invalid.

Clouds, land.

Rain, eating.

Meadow.

Males twice a female's weight, plus drought, the kochia good, and opinion after Line's tampering, with advocates for both sides and her expulsion moderate. Why would a random intervene from abroad? Who is she to combat the natural forces of the country's climate? Why be here? Line only reaps the harvest for herself among hock, muzzle, horns long in clouds to stoke a flood hostile above the car, where the hooves fly along the roof like bells, the instinct to ban either woman from anywhere—freedom for all as a barnstorm—even though Line's falling into park across the blacktop toward ballots much quieter than asphalt's rasp—people, few, mum in the booths of a lobby, psychosis.

Debate.

Among legislators, whose dribble must throw the free from court? By nudging baselines over a ton, the window of a rigged match appears legal upon reflection, foul and to an extreme center without any opinion except what's carrying gravity, scandal transparent, felt.

How then might the immigrant hone new ideas without being called out of bounds?

She must prod on, keeping with PROPOSITION 1:

Ordinances will create city when a boulevard's open lean invites character, that nice place where we hang out in sunlight's umami above the nag about skyscrapers, which could overshadow precious views, whatever, of conserving homelessness.

Gentrification.

Under new roofs, Line may evacuate her tenement. But to punch down? Voting against the measure throws water on sleeping bags. Since she's alone, the answers crop up as her own interpretation of red, blue, green, and pink slime.

Skyscrapers would darken her own shadow even during the day.

"Hello, can explain or not?"

"What's the matter?" a poll worker says.

"This not in my country."

"Must be a beautiful place. Basically, higher income earners start riding poor neighborhoods. It makes people angry because they grew up in a museum. Like places should prioritize those who were born there by chance. Bullshit. If we go back a thousand years, nobody belongs. We're conquerors. The real problem's a lack of building. Contractors constrain the land."

"Less building, no gentry fiction?"

"In my opinion. Everyone has their own thing about everything."

Another worker helps Line after that one leaves. "I can explain it better. Gentrification's about corporate willpower. If you live in a cheap unit, financiers and bankers and hedge funds—they'd make less. So these condominiums and McMansions, they're roping us in. Have you seen new developments? I live in a luxury unit and hear the doorman ten floors below."

That worker leaves when someone else spies intimidation.

"It's about incentives," a third says. "You'd need to live here for a while to get a handle on it because, like, corporations give. All people need a purpose in life, and business generates the means. I'm not a murderer, but I'd toke, and I'd lay about without a job. I'd just fuck. Honest. But I never tell. It's fine to slouch, but society'll stop. I dissemble. Yeah, property taxes also. City needs money. City collects."

Does Line agree or disagree?

She selects an answer, defining the word herself.

PROPOSITION 2:

Guns control the narrative and reduce freedom if blood's shed opens. Many tools: the mad cow disease regarding the defense of our nation as justice in spite of school shootings, the boy's face blown off at a gender reveal party.

In Line's native land, few can even search for weapons out beyond law. Anything sharp has round length.

Amend the necrophilia.

Take away the nation's rebels.

Ban them.

Yet aren't big, muscular cars more the weaponry?

Great harms pass by drivers, beefy, metallic bulls romping over roadkill, and still the streets go full with empty stomachs acidifying our atmosphere at enough speed to pick up groceries, visit friends, house garages for other vehicles, no duty to retreat.

Compromise. Everyone can walk away engines running. Locals say if they arm themselves politely then politeness is just given.

Self-defense.

Allow for roaming.

Roam wherever.

Nice, akin to chopping off a foot for the weep instead of chopping an onion, which most would prefer, yet here they enjoy the massacre, opinion's slaughterhouse grinding the extremities to paper.

PROPOSITION 3:

Ruby's finishing up a question. She had to have chosen YES on PROP 1, though if you select yes, does it mean yes to yes, yes to maybe, or yes to no? A third of the room may label yes no, and the other half could no yes, and the final quarter I HATE POLITICS.

Childish thought, perish; however, living here's rubbernecking, what with decisions under the influence of growth hormones.

PROPOSITION 4:

Should we even greet each other anymore? Bacteria grow when palms clam together out of respect for customs to boss society around, finger in the handshake of a firm among the interviews.

Careerism: an exclusionary policy predicated on the ladder's rung farther than the next but equally spaced out for appearances.

Yet what involves the habitual?

An insult.

We're insulting each other's privacy by contaminating respect. If you gift a sweater, the recipient accepts extra heat, and spectra emit what we perceive.

She's not colorblind though.

Even teeth stimulate the flash of unequal: a hello hurts. In theory, the act spreads serotonin, but what if you're allergic to the hive mind's bread? Are kisses worthless normie fiction?

Line would never mean to denigrate anyone.

She's most inclusive.

Therefore, culture is nonconsensual.

How the country sickens from steak tartare, for chefs marble even our president's diet to sanction the heartland, fields of grease serving up anthem: illusion, claims of fraudulent data in the cook book's carbon neutral prime cut. If the forage and feedlot go, Line'll fork another flank whose superpower focuses on jobs, the economy, stupid, model the pasture she swoons after, with Ruby in podcast, unplugging the break. "What's wrong? What's the matter?"

"Everything's everything. Anything's everything. Everything's anything," Line says. "Show the last question? Some answer. Ah, must be the milk."

"They had water, soda, and Kool-Aid. Putting yourself in danger, what kind of psychopath are you?"

Line tells her.

"Really? I wouldn't have thought. You're more open-minded than me. Unwashed leaves," Ruby says, "leave behind stranger meat."

"From any greens?"

"In hamburgers."

"Can vomit outside? Where? Where?"

"Here, here." In a doggie bag thin across the ground, nuggets and fries, the master-planned community rafting peas wet with splatter by half eats, fresh chicken over an outcrop of lettuce icebergs adrift into a warm cheese grove where tomatoes wrinkle plastic reflection—goo on pavement an allure for citizens concerned about the ordeal inside, the innards a template any might feel after quorum. "Ain't no stopping her," Ruby says. "She only ate one hamburger, and the world's like this. Y'all watch her go ham next."

A Farmworker's Ballad

Elise Swanson Ochoa

Green. Green, go. *Gringo*. Some say the word came from the Mexican's scoffed "*véte, verde,*" glaring at the straight green stripe of the uniform worn by the mustached men invading their country. Like an old western, '*get out, green one,*' with a spitball in the direction of the devil. Well, the *gringos* won that war. Now? They still fight dirty. The red, the blue, the old against their own young. Blood money is muscle. They cheat and thank *Gee-zus*. *Ay*, but they hate *Hey-sus*; they don't see him. Then they'd have to pay him, he'd have earned something, a seat at the table. How they demand that salad on their plate. So green. So crisp. So cheap, thanks to *my* back and *my* hands. My muddy hands cradle my soft, brown baby girl. Those *gringos* will tell anyone their crystal glass and silver fork are worth more than she. They stuff their ruddy faces with the meticulously cultivated fruits of the earth. Green grow. Green, go.

Žižek at the In–N–Out

Taylor Greene

I don't know how to tell you what you already know.
There's an orbit, between you and I
circling 'round and 'round
between your milkshake and my fries.
A salty snack in a sweet treat, and you smile at me
as I steal a dip,
but you won't kiss me
while my mouth is full of Marx and revelation.
That's fine by me.

What to Do to Go to Hell

Andrea Caswell

We bought coffee and gasoline at a truck stop in Nebraska. The Sapp Bros. sign—a giant blue metal coffee pot—rose like a beacon over the interstate, the eternal I-80 East leading us back to Boston. As intended, the sign's old-timey pot with a spout suggested Sapp Bros. had been in the coffee business a long time, and perhaps they have. I asked my husband to pull in there instead of at the millionth McDonald's we'd passed.

It's hard not to get your hopes up about what may await at one of these road stops. You're desperate to be surprised after a thousand miles of wheat-colored monotony. Ever since I'd missed my chance to enjoy "Homemade Pies" at a diner in Vale, Oregon two days earlier, I'd been craving fresh baked goods. Maybe Sapp Bros. would have patented cinnamon rolls, or warm apple donuts steaming up a glass case.

Brown tile. Blackened grout. A tub of Slim Jims by the cash register. How foolish to have imagined anything more than the standard candy selection and a shiny, rolling hot-dog machine. Week-old Fresh Sandwiches smothered in plastic wrap. Soda and cigarettes. Everything and nothing.

I headed to the self-service coffee area, with my hope somehow still intact. *Maybe this will be the best coffee ever*, I thought. There were three varieties on tap: the "Smile" blend (A Beautifully Smooth Roast); "Awake" (Infused with Extra Caffeine to Keep You Focused); and the unusual "Decaf Smile." I filled two cups with an inexact combination of Smile and Awake, anything to mix it up for the push across Nebraska. Then the creamer decision, French Vanilla or plain. That's when a handwritten sign caught my eye, a piece of cardboard wedged against the Sweet 'N Low rack. *Free Bibles*. Arranged on a wooden shelf on the counter were ten identical books with red plastic covers, not as big as the ones in hotel bedside tables, but not miniature ones, either.

You know that weird impulse to take anything that's free, just because it's free? I'm not religious, but writers are supposed to read every single thing they can get their hands on, right? In college I'd wanted to take a class called "The Bible as Literature," but it conflicted with Beginning Italian, more romantic and impractical, my *modus operandi*. Then I noticed another free item in the bookcase. It was a pamphlet called *What to Do to Go to HELL*. I grabbed one and slid it into my purse, and that stealthy motion made me feel like I was stealing something.

Back at the RV, it was my turn to drive. "Any baked goods?" my husband asked. Ward knew about my pie remorse.

"No. But they had a bunch of bibles. I actually passed up a free book."

"You?"

"I got this instead." I gave him the pamphlet and asked him to read it aloud as we drove. Almost anything passes for entertainment on a five-week road trip.

He read the title dramatically, like the announcer of a cheesy game show. It wasn't quite game-show material, though.

"Alrighty then," he said. This topic was out of character for me, a person more likely to take brochures with titles like *Juicing for Life!* and *Choosing Paint Colors*.

The pamphlet was printed on slick magazine paper with a black background. *HELL* was in all caps, and the word was partially obscured by orange flames, as if the pamphlet itself were catching on fire. Ward opened it to the answer, the what-to-do part.

First there was silence. Eventually he said, "It doesn't say anything."

I assumed he was joking, withholding the punchline to prolong the read-aloud. We had another 1800 miles to go before Boston. "What do you mean?" I asked.

"I mean, it's blank inside." He held it up so I could see it easily, without taking my eyes from the road for too long. White space on the paper, as white as the cottony clouds hanging over the Heartland.

I wasn't just disappointed. I felt crestfallen, as if I'd missed the chance to learn something crucial for me to know. I wondered if maybe this one leaflet was defective—a misprint—and presumed the answers awaited in the other ones, still sitting on the shelf at Sapp Bros., now in our rearview mirror.

Ward closed the leaflet and flipped it over to the backside. "But wait, there's more!" he said as TV-announcer-man. He read the words printed on the back. "Nothing! There is absolutely nothing we need to do to go to Hell."

I asked him to read it again; I still thought he was joking or making it up. He continued: *"All have sinned—there is none that doeth good—he that believeth not is condemned already (John 3:18)."*

How unhelpful. The title of the pamphlet had sounded so authoritative—a printed version of clickbait—yet it was useless. The truth is, I wanted a tangible answer, maybe with a specific list of do's and don't's. But why did I want that so badly, and from a free brochure at a truck stop, no less? What about my own belief system?

I knew what I believed, mainly that 'heaven' and 'hell' are here on Earth, inside of us. They're not lurking off in the future somewhere, but here and now. We can experience them—these inner emotional states—at any time, not so much because of morally charged acts, but because we have faults and blind spots. Moments of weakness. We make mistakes.

I sometimes wonder what I'd go back and change if I could. It's a futile question, coated in regret, but

I can't shake it. We're all in possession of a time machine—the brain—which allows us to replay our lives, but only as observers, never as agents with the benefit of hindsight. Confusingly, most of what I'd change is the same as what I wouldn't change, such as my first marriage. I'd like to have made better decisions for myself, yet I wouldn't undo it, because it's why I have my two daughters. I've noticed I look back more frequently now, after passing a milestone-birthday, 50. Usually I contemplate what I did wrong instead of the victories. My mother told me never to rest on past laurels, so my mind steers toward the brambles. The thorns.

A day earlier, before entering Nebraska, we drove through Wyoming, in a northward swing through the snow-capped Grand Tetons, then southeast to connect with I-80. We stopped in Laramie for gas, then continued off the highway another ten miles or so, winding our way into the Laramie Mountains. That night—the night before Nebraska and the brochure—we made camp next to Crystal Lake in Curt Gowdy State Park, where the clean scent of pine trees filled the wind. Outcroppings of boulders dominated the landscape and red rocks were strewn across high prairies, as if a giant had been playing with marbles. Being there made me think of my oldest daughter, Desiree. In high school, she'd acted in "The Laramie Project," a play about the murder of University of Wyoming student Matthew Shepard. I wondered if this beautiful place we'd decided to camp was near where he'd been killed. It had to be.

And I remembered one afternoon before the play,

when Desiree, about fifteen years old, had asked if I wanted my name in the *Parent Patrons* section of the program. Each cast member was required to sell a certain amount of space to fundraise. In whatever way she'd asked the question, my answer was quick and harsh, something like, *I've already given enough money to the drama department.* It had cost maybe $60 for her to participate in the play, less than a trip to the grocery store. I still cringe at that knee-jerk response, at my careless refusal, even though I wasn't making ends meet at the time.

The opening night of the play, I felt so proud of her. In the buzzing auditorium, reading the program while waiting for the lights to dim, I perused the *Parent Patrons*, each listed as a $10 supporter. *Only ten dollars?* Desiree hadn't told me that, and I'd like to think that I could have—would have—spared ten dollars. But the fact is, I hadn't given her the chance to tell me. I shut her down and shut her out, with the smug notion that I'd already done enough. Though I claim I wasn't making ends meet, I routinely spent ten dollars on cigarettes and a loser-boyfriend and all-natural dog food. But for some reason on that afternoon, I wasn't generous enough or loving enough to support my beautiful daughter.

I run that scene through the time machine, as well as the night I spent in Laramie, ruminating about regrets. I think I've pieced together what I needed at the Sapp Bros. stop in Nebraska. I'd grabbed that brochure in hopes of finding easy answers to difficult questions. I craved a quick serving of whether I was *good* or *bad*, instead of having to grapple with a lifetime of experiences—all the messiness of maternal guilt, and the sadness of my first marriage ending in divorce. Wisdom, such as understanding we don't fit into simplistic categories like *good* and *bad*, is earned, not free. We even use language like *hard-won*, as if we're fighting a battle, and maybe we are as we sort through the wreckage of our own humanity. Amidst the pieces, wedged between the bitter and the sweet, is the possibility we'll be surprised by what we find.

scene

C.C. Rayne

front car of the train:
a cowboy, lounging.
(that's the word. *lounging.*)

hat-brim pulled down over shaded frown,
shirt open four buttons deep,
brass-bound belt, boots the color of a sandstorm.

the sound: whir-groan of gears, plus a faint snore.

and the world through the window:
bright red streaks of sand, sky like a blue neon sign.
a great wide wildness of desert beyond the curtain,
strange creatures sprinting fast beside the train car,
left eventually in the dust.

rainbow blur through crushed-crystal windowglass
slows, grows,
forms itself into a station:
one of the grey ones, inconsequential,
place with a name like *Bray* or *Melvie* or *Shalmaloo*
that no one cares for.
no one disembarks—
save for: a cowboy.
passengers clutch luggage and watch subtly from the
benches.
he approaches the ticket window.
looking to go somewhere? says the icy pretty clerk.
the frown stays bolted to the man's lovely mouth.

always looking, ma'am, but never finding.

there should be a sunset behind him. something to
frame the words,
and cast him in shadow.
instead, there is steady rain. acid water. his boots
won't hold for long.
this place was not meant for him to find.

gallop apace

C.C. Rayne

there is a ranger in need of rescue.
name's *cadentia.*
(funny name).

deep in the desert, the cowboy rides
rough-shod; horse-hooves kick dust
into his eyes. he pulls his hat down further.
a new coat—stour and thick, not glamorous,
but the sun scorches and the nights are deadly cold.
what use is glamor on a skeleton?
no lounging here.
away from the eyes of the world,
the sky is sickening. it stretches out out out up out
up above.

and one day, the cowboy looks up too long.
gets dazzled by the half-sphere liquid-lake, same
shade as a beetle's back—

—he slips from his saddle—

the impact is small,
dull and angry.
blackness.
a day later, he wakes up to vultures,
fights 'em off with the buckle of his belt.
grimly counts the chamber for remaining bullets.
that poster was pretty old. that cry for help might
well be moot.
why not go back? to the station, to the train?

wanna find something new is the answer.
a half-answer - loneliness, the full.
but whatever lies one tells oneself for the sake of a
good thing
are counted well in the sight of the sky.

the cowboy starts walking.

days, into nights, into more days.
no skin visible, between the broad-brimmed hat and
long-sleeved coat.
a living shadow, lost 'midst red-blood dust.

It Can Come Again

Shelby Hinte

We are road tripping towards the Santa Cruz Mountains for your brother's 50th birthday. We left after work, after dinner, to avoid the traffic. It's dark over the valley which is as flat as the cow shit that stinks up the air. If you weren't from around here, you wouldn't know how close you are to the ocean, to tie-dye loving hippies with too much money, to frat boys who barf on the boardwalk. This stretch of highway is just another California contradiction.

"Fuck," you say, interrupting the country song I've put on for the drive.

"What is it?"

"Fuck. Fuck. Fuck." You are clenching the steering wheel and won't look at me. You are in your own head. I know this look. I have seen it enough times in the last seven years to know what it means.

"You forget your doses?" You don't look at me, but I can tell just by the way your face twitches that you have.

"I'm such a fucking idiot."

"Hey, don't talk about my husband like that." I try to take your hand in mine, to console you, but I also kind of think you are a fucking idiot. A better wife wouldn't admit this, but it is nearly ten pm and we are an hour away from home, an hour away from our destination, and I don't want to turn back now.

"We have to turn back."

"Yeah."

"Are you mad?"

"I'll drive us to the cabin."

"You don't have to."

"I don't want you to have to drive four hours. That's silly."

"Thanks."

I look in the backseat and see our kid still sleeping. He won't know the difference.

This is not the first time this has happened—your doses getting in the way of our life plans. Once, three years ago, on a camping trip for my birthday, we had to leave a day earlier than everyone else because you hadn't earned enough take-homes from the clinic. You'd been pissing clean. You'd been banking on your counselor making an exception for my birthday. He hadn't.

I was less forgiving then. I wasn't yet "in recovery." I didn't even think I had a real problem. This is easy to do when the person you're with has a more ostensible problem.

206

I was a queen at rationalizing the difference in our using—*I never used needles, I could go long stretches with only drinking and not drugging, I never spent my portion of rent on a bender.* I wasn't thinking of all the ways my own using had inconvenienced you. How it made me quick to anger. How it made me paranoid you'd leave me. How I'd beg you to tell me over and over again you'd never leave me because I couldn't hear it the first time through all the substances in my blood. No, at the time, I was only thinking of how we had to leave before everyone else, about how even in sobriety your addiction was ruining my birthday. I chugged three beers back-to-back in the morning before having to sit in the car next to you on the drive home. I picked little fights with you about it for weeks afterwards.

I like to think I'm a more understanding wife now. Less quick to anger. Not as paranoid you'll leave me. At least not as vocal about it.

The last time you forgot your doses was the 4th of July two years ago. By then I was sober too—just a couple months. It wasn't until we were a day into our trip that you realized you'd left your doses above the fridge in the little lock box the clinic made you carry. We were staying with your brother and his new boyfriend Matt, who, it turned out, has chronic pain and a government funded pharmacy of all our favorite pills to go with it. Matt's morning ritual is to smoke a joint and take a fistful of pill with his coffee. I have often wondered if your brother, who was so intolerant of your using days, has ever questioned the behaviors of his own boyfriend. Matt knows we're sober but that doesn't stop him from offering us pills every time we wince when standing from the couch or massage the parts of our bodies that suffer from aging. Our suffering is one that cannot be so easily subdued.

Whenever we've been offered pills, to my knowledge, we have both always declined the offer. I imagine we have both also privately wanted to sneak into his room and stuff a handful of his pills in our pockets to relapse in secret.

On that 4th of July trip, you'd just hit three years sober. It was the morning after we'd arrived when you realized that you'd forgotten your doses.

"Shit," you'd said, pacing around the room and tapping your palm against your forehead like you could will a solution into existence.

"It's just one more day," I said. I tried to sound calm, but I was just as afraid as you, thinking about the way your body would be drenched in sweat within a couple of hours, thinking about the way it would cloud your thought, and even though I wasn't the biggest fan of you taking those doses from the clinic to stay sober, I knew what life had looked like without them.

"I could just ask Matt for a Vicodin," you said, looking across the room at me. I'd been sitting on the bed watching you pace and going through my own mental gymnastics to try and find a way to finish the weekend out without going home early, without risking your sobriety, without watching you crawl in your own skin from opiate withdrawal.

"I could just take one, just to manage," you said.

You had stopped pacing. You looked at me, waiting for me for me to give permission.

"That is a terrible fucking idea."

"I don't think it's as bad as you think."

"This is scaring me."

"Seriously?"

"You can't go a couple fucking hours?"

"You don't know what it's like."

I didn't say anything because I knew you couldn't really believe this, but maybe you did. I think I know you, know what's best, but I don't live inside your body. I stubbornly stick with the memories of my own withdrawals. I project them onto your experience. I can be like this sometimes. Assuming I know everything. It is my least favorite thing about myself. It is an unlovable quality. You love me anyway. That you love me anyway means I will never leave you. Not even if you ask Matt for a Vicodin. Not even if it leads everything else. Not even if it took me with you.

It's the *everything else* I was thinking about when you suggested asking Matt for a pill. I know you aren't the kind of person who can have just one of something. I know it because I'm not either.

The first thing to come to mind whenever I think of a relapse is your last relapse. Funny how we never get rid of those old memories, how they just grow and grow and grow over time. It was so long ago now. It feels unfair that the image of it—you sleeping in the car out front of our home, me crying alone in the house changing the locks, thinking my great love story might have come to an end—has superseded other more pleasant images.

Sometimes I think we are both just collecting days together in hopes that the accumulation of newer, better images, will finally wipe away all the bad ones. It only makes sense that this should happen, given the sheer volume of pleasant images to choose from.

In the end, we didn't spend the holiday with your brother and Matt. You feigned ill, which wasn't too far from the truth. There was no relapse. We packed up the car with our barely opened bags and headed home.

On the drive home, our son didn't stop asking why. We were supposed to go swimming, eat hot dogs, drink soda, do other all-American type shit like a normal family. He was disappointed. You drove and every time I looked over at you, I could see you hating yourself. Your jaw clenched. Your fingers tight around the steering wheel. The way you wouldn't take your eyes off the road to join the conversation.

"Let's order pizza and have a movie marathon tonight," I said.

"Yes!" Our son said from the backseat.

Now, we are on the highway headed towards the Santa Cruz Mountains for a weekend trip with your brother and Matt. We don't ever say it out loud, but I know these trips always have us both a little more on edge than normal. They are like a test, asking, *have you really changed? Do you really want it?* I like to think the answer is *yes,* but I can only ever speak for myself, and you can never know for certain what I am thinking.

"Fuck," you say again, and I coo and say it is

going to be okay. I bring my index finger to my lip to remind you of our son asleep in the backseat. It is late on a Friday night, and we are both exhausted from a full week of work, childrearing, attempting to maintain sanity and sobriety. You change lanes and we are pulling off the freeway to get back on in the other direction towards home. I am annoyed, but I try not to let it show. I am always thinking of how much kinder you were to me when I got sober than I was to you when you got sober. You never made me sleep in the car in our driveway or changed the locks, and so I am repaying my debt by keeping my mouth shut when I'm annoyed. I think kindness comes so much more naturally to you than it does to me.

It is for the best that you remembered the doses tonight and not in the morning when we are with everyone at the cabin. Matt will be there this weekend with his pharmacy of pills, and we need all the help we can get. We always need all the help we can get.

I turn the country song up so we don't have to talk.

I saw the light
I've been baptized
By the fire in your touch
And the flame in your eyes

When we get back to the house, we leave the car running so we don't startle our kid awake. We both go in, you for your doses and me for my Diet Cokes. I take one from the fridge and chug it in the halo of the open fridge. I crush the can and toss it into the recycling, grab two more for the road. We won't get to the cabin until after 2am now. The sodas will keep me awake, maybe help make me feel some way different than the way I feel.

We have to get gas on the way out of town and our son opens his eyes from the backseat when we turn the car off beneath the bright fluorescent lights of the gas station.

"Are we home?"

"Yeah."

"Why?"

"We forgot something, but we are on our way now."

He nods. Closes his eyes. Falls back asleep.

We pull onto the dark stretch of backroad that leads out of town and you reach across the center console and take my hand in yours.

"Hey," you say, and I look over at you, your face is in the shadow of night, but I can see your eyes searching mine, "I'm sorry."

"I know." I squeeze your hand. "I love you." I wait for you to say it back. You do. It carries me across the darkest stretch of highway.

Allyn Bernkopf
Andrea Caswell
August Edwards
C.C. Rayne
Dee Engan
Devon Bohm
Elise Swanson Ochoa
Emily Nelson
Evan Nicholls
Evan Williams
Harriet Prebble
J. Robert Lennon
Justin Taylor
Kate Finegan
Katie Manning
Lindsay Hunter
Margaret Grayson
Matthew Medendorp
Max Dougherty
Maya Lowy
Mike Nagel
Rebecca Ferrier
Sage Marshall
Sarah Lyn Rogers
Shelby Hinte
Taylor Greene
Tina S. Zhu

ALLYN BERNKOPF is a Ph.D. Candidate in English, Poetry at Oklahoma State University, where she was the recipient of the Gladys Burris Creative Writing Fellowship, and is an Associate Editor for The Cimarron Review. Her work has appeared or is forthcoming in Foothill Poetry Journal, Rock & Sling, Barzakh Magazine, Bayou Magazine, Two Thirds North Magazine, The Greensboro Review, Door = Jar, Open Minds Quarterly, and others, and has been anthologized in Women's Voices Anthology (These Fragile Lilacs 2017) and Lost: Reflections (Medusa's Laugh Press, 2017). She holds a Master of Arts in English from Weber State University.

ANDREA CASWELL holds an MFA in fiction and nonfiction from the Bennington Writing Seminars. She's a senior fiction editor at Cleaver Magazine and is on the faculty of the Cleaver Workshops. Her work appears or is forthcoming in Tampa Review, The Coachella Review, River Teeth, The Normal School, Columbia Journal, and others. She's an alum of the Sewanee Writers' Conference and has been nominated for a Pushcart Prize. For more information, please visit www.andreacaswell.com.

AUGUST EDWARDS is the founder of Albuquerque Green Room and the nonfiction and art editor for Fourteen Hills. You can find her work in Mulberry Literary, Glyph, Hard Noise, and Entropy.

C.C. RAYNE is a writer, musician, and actor based on the East Coast of the USA. An avid lover of all things weird, discontented, and out-of-place, C.C.'s work seeks to blend the magical with the mundane.

DEE ENGAN is a writer. Learn more at deeengan.com.

DEVON BOHM received her BA from Smith College and earned her MFA with a dual concentration in Poetry and Fiction from Fairfield University. She has been awarded the Hatfield Prize for Best Short Story, was longlisted for Wigleaf's Top Very Short Fictions, and has received two honorable mentions in L. Ron Hubbard Writers of the Future Contest— winning the contest in the 2nd Quarter of 2022. Her work has also been featured in publications such as Labrys, The Graveyard Zine, Horse Egg Literary, Necessary Fiction, Eunoia Review, Spry, Sixfold, Hole In The Head Review, orangepeel, Helix Magazine, Sunday Mornings at the River's 365 Days of Covid anthology, and is upcoming in boats against the current and Discretionary Love. Her first book of poetry, Careful Cartography, was published in November 2021 by Cornerstone Press as part of their Portage

Poetry series. The collection was the recipient of the 2022 First Horizons Book Award and was shortlisted for the 2022 Eric Hoffer Award, receiving the distinction for an outstanding publication by an academic press. Follow her on Instagram or TikTok @devonpoem or visit her website at www.devonbohm.com.

ELISE SWANSON OCHOA'S work has been featured or is forthcoming in Allium, Five on the Fifth, The Loch Raven Review, Los Angeles Poets for Justice, The Opiate, Packingtown Review, Potato Soup Journal, Word West Revue, and Wrath-Bearing Tree. She holds a BA in Spanish and linguistics from UCLA and a Doctor of Optometry degree from Southern California College of Optometry. Elise is an optometrist in Santa Barbara.

EMILY NELSON is a writer from the Pacific Northwest currently pursuing an MFA in Fiction at the University of Montana. Her writing has been published in The Rumpus, Ayaskala, and Drizzle Review, and has received support from Tin House and Bread Loaf.

EVAN NICHOLLS is a poet and collage artist from Virginia. His work appears or is forthcoming in DIAGRAM, Guesthouse, Hobart and HAD, among others. He is the author of a chapbook of poems and collages, Holy Smokes, and one of the minds behind the micro-chap THERE HAS BEEN A MURDER, co-written with Evan Williams and Benjamin Niespodziany. Both books are available from Ghost City Press. Find more of his work at enicholls.com.

EVAN WILLIAMS is a Chicago-based writer interested in the collision of surrealism and the natural world. Their poetry and fiction have appeared in DIAGRAM, Indiana Review, and Pleiades, among others. Evan is a co-founding editor of Obliterat, the temporary journal of prose poetry, and a contributing writer for the Cleveland Review of Books.

HARRIET PREBBLE is a writer, performer and gamer from Ōtautahi, Aotearoa. She has an enduring fascinating for sad cowboys across all mediums.

J. ROBERT LENNON is the author of nine novels, including Familiar, Broken River, and Subdivision, and the story collections Pieces for the Left Hand, See You in Paradise, and Let Me Think. He lives in Ithaca, New York.

JUSTIN TAYLOR is the author of the memoir Riding with the Ghost, (Random House in 2020) as well as three books of fiction published by HarperCollins: Everything Here Is the Best Thing Ever (2010), The Gospel of Anarchy (2011), and Flings (2014). His next novel, Reboot, is forthcoming from Pantheon in 2024. His work has appeared in The New Yorker, Harper's, Bomb, and Bookforum, among other publications. He has taught writing at the graduate and undergraduate level in programs all over the country, including Columbia University, N.Y.U., the University of Southern Mississippi, and the University of Montana. He is the Director of the Sewanee School of Letters. He lives in Portland, Oregon.

KATE FINEGAN (she/her) is a writer and editor living on Treaty Six territory in Edmonton. Learn more at katefinegan.ink.

KATIE MANNING is the founding editor-in-chief of Whale Road Review and a professor of writing at Point Loma Nazarene University in San Diego. She's the author of Tasty Other, which won the 2016 Main Street Rag Poetry Book Award, and her most recent chapbooks are How to Play (Louisiana Literature Press, 2022) and 28,065 Nights (River Glass Books, 2020). Her poems have appeared in American Journal of Nursing, december, The Lascaux Review, New Letters, Poet Lore, Thimble, and many other venues. Find her on Twitter @iamkatmann.

LINDSAY HUNTER is the author of two story collections and two novels. Her most recent novel, Eat Only When You're Hungry, was a Book of the Month Club selection, a finalist for the 2017 Chicago Review of Books Fiction Award, and a 2017 NPR Great Read. Her next book, a novel titled Hot Springs Drive, is forthcoming on Roxane Gay Books in November 2023. She lives in Chicago with her family.

MARGARET GRAYSON is an essayist and journalist from southwest Colorado. She graduated from the University of Montana School of Journalism and is an MFA candidate at Washington University in St. Louis. She's the 2022 winner of the Montana Quarterly's Big Snowy Prize for Nonfiction.

MATTHEW MEDENDORP is a poet and essayist with an MFA from Northern Arizona University. He lives in Brooklyn, Michigan—a town that confuses people who don't read through the end of a sentence. You can read more of his work in Hobart, Essay Daily, and at mattmedendorp.com

MAX DOUGHERTY (he/him) is a transgender man living in Seattle with his two cats, Sawyer and Oliver. Max works in healthcare with the intent to create a more navigable environment and picked up writing again several years after graduating from the University of Chicago with a minor in creative writing. He does not remember when he started writing poetry, but still has memorized the first poem he published as a kid.

Born and raised in Santa Cruz, California, MAYA LOWY received her MFA in poetry at the University of New Orleans in 2016 and currently lives in Gloucestershire, UK, with her husband and dog. Her work can be found in Bacopa Literary Review, Triggerfish Critical Review, Sweet: A Literary Confection, Infection House, and other publications. She tweets @apurpleyam.

MIKE NAGEL is the author of Duplex (Autofocus Books, 2022). Find selected nonsense at michaelscottnagel.com.

REBECCA FERRIER won the Bridge Award in 2020 and funding for her first lyrical novel from Creative Scotland in 2021. Her recent poetry has been published in Lighthouse, Siegfried's Journal, Paradox Literary and The Heather Anthology of Scottish Art and Poetry. Her latest prose can be found with Gutter (Issue 25) and Channel. Twitter/Instagram: @rmlferrier

SAGE MARSHALL is an essayist and poet, who daylights as an editor for Field & Stream, and writes creative work whenever he can. His creative essays have been featured in publications such as The Missouri Review, Sport Literate, and Reverberations Magazine. His poems have found homes in Arc Poetry Magazine, The Appalachian Review, Emerge Literary Journal, The Boulder Weekly, and elsewhere. His work was named notable in Best American Essays 2021. He is currently working on a book-length project called 'The Barbs' that delves into the intersections of ice hockey, the outdoors, the West, boyhood, violence, and masculinity.

SARAH LYN ROGERS is an NYC-based writer from the San Francisco Bay Area. She edits books for Soft Skull Press and is the series co-editor for the anthology Best Debut Short Stories: The PEN America Dau Prize. She is the author of the chapbooks Inevitable What (Sad Spell Press, 2016) and Autocorrect Suggests "Tithe" (Ghost City Press, 2021), with poems published or forthcoming at HAD, Hobart, Dream Pop, and

Witch Craft Mag. Sarah was the 2014 winner of the Academy of American Poets' Virginia de Araujo Prize, and a finalist for the 2019 St. Lawrence Book Award. For more of Sarah's work, visit sarahlynrogers.com.

SHELBY HINTE is the Associate Editor of Write or Die Magazine and a prose reader for No Contact. She has volunteered at various small presses including ZYZZYVA, Split/Lip Press. Her writing has appeared in BOMB magazine, SmokeLong Quarterly, ZYZZYVA, Hobart, HAD, Bending Genres, and elsewhere. She lives in Northern California.

TAYLOR GREENE is an archeologist working in Arkansas, which means spends more time reading than you'd think. You can find some of his other work in the anthologies Hell is Real and Mid/South. You can find him on Instagram as @vert_archy.

TINA S. ZHU writes from her dining table in NYC. Her work has appeared in X-R-A-Y, Sundog Lit, and The Journal of Compressed Creative Arts, among other places. She can be found at tinaszhu.com.

word west revue

wordwestrevue.co